PAPAL ENFORCEMENT OF SOME MEDIEVAL MARRIAGE LAWS

Papal Enforcement of
SOME MEDIEVAL
MARRIAGE LAWS

CHARLES EDWARD SMITH, Ph.D.
ASSOCIATE PROFESSOR OF HISTORY
LOUISIANA STATE UNIVERSITY

LOUISIANA STATE UNIVERSITY PRESS
UNIVERSITY : LOUISIANA : 1940

PREFACE

This study is a revision of a dissertation submitted to the Department of History and the Graduate School of the University of Pennsylvania in partial fulfillment of the requirements for the doctorate.

I am particularly indebted to Dr. A. C. Howland, Professor of Medieval History at the University of Pennsylvania, for his many kindnesses and his constantly helpful guidance in the preparation of this monograph. Professor Edward P. Cheyney likewise made a number of valuable suggestions for the improvement of the content and style, and I greatly appreciate his interest. Professor Loren C. MacKinney of the University of North Carolina also read the manuscript critically and gave pertinent advice for its improvement. I am in no way relieved, however, of full responsibility for errors of fact or judgment.

In gathering material for this study I was fortunate to enjoy access to the Henry Charles Lea Library of Medieval History at the University of Pennsylvania. I also wish to express my appreciation to the librarians and staffs of the libraries of Harvard University, Yale University, University of Chicago, Princeton University, the University of Michigan, and the Library of Congress. I also was the recipient of courtesies from the Library of the British Museum and the Bibliothèque Nationale. I am indebted to Mr. James A. McMillen, Director of Libraries at the Louisiana State University, and members of his staff.

Mr. Fred C. Cole has given invaluable assistance in preparing the manuscript for printing.

Hefele has been cited where it contains the Latin text of the canons dealing with marital impediments. Where the text is not given either in Hefele or in Hefele-Leclerq, the citation is to Mansi.

C. E. S.

University, Louisiana
November 1, 1939

CONTENTS

INTRODUCTION

The canon law postulates that marriage is divinely ordained for the propagation of the race and the nurture of love and charity. A man and woman enter into a permanent contractual relationship, and mutual consent is therefore a prime essential for marital union.

From the nature of marriage it is apparent that there are circumstances and conditions which preclude a valid contract, since requisite physical, mental, or spiritual qualities are absent in either or both parties. Such conditions or circumstances are termed impediments; unless dispensation is secured they prevent marriage or enforce the separation of those ostensibly married.

An impediment may be of either the *impedientia* or the *dirimentia* type. The former prevents marriage, while the latter nullifies a union already concluded. An impediment may be present at the time of the marriage or may arise subsequent to it. It may be temporary or permanent, publicly known or secret.

A number of impediments preclude the free mutual consent which is a *sine qua non* of the marital relationship. One or both of the parties may lack the mental faculties necessary for a binding contract because of immaturity, insanity, inebriation, hypnotic influence, or other factors. Misunderstanding of the nature and purpose of marriage also is an impediment. For example, if the parties fail to understand the permanent and monogamous nature of the marital union or do not realize that procreation is a primary objective, this impediment would arise.

Error in person or quality likewise precludes a valid marriage. Mistaken identity obviously would be incompatible with free consent. A man might learn after marriage that his wife was opposed to the rearing of offspring, and this would be grounds for nullity since a quality necessary for marriage is absent. Lack of consent also may be the result of a simulated intent to marry, or due to the assumption that a civil ceremony is sufficient. Nonfulfillment of a proper and attainable condition may be grounds for a declaration of nullity, but it may not be if the condition understood at the time of the marriage is incompatible with the nature of the marital union.

Force and fear operate to prevent consent. Duress naturally is irreconcilable with conclusion of a marital union, and fear, if sufficiently justified to bring about wavering of mind and spirit in a normal person, likewise may preclude free consent. Rape is an impediment, as is impotence which prevents the performance of the procreative act. Sterility cannot be taken as *prima facie* evidence of the existence of the impediment of impotence.

Vows of celibacy and ordination to the priesthood in the four highest grades prevent marriage or enforce separation. Adultery is ground for nullity in that it violates the basic, monogamous nature of the marital union. Disparity of cult arises if one of the parties to a marriage is unbaptized or not baptized according to the teaching of the Church. Failure to conform to the usages and

forms prescribed by the Church engenders the impediment of clandestinity.

Relationship between the parties within prescribed
limits constitutes a *dirimentia* or *impedientia* impediment. Although incestuous unions between near relatives
are well-nigh universally abhorred, rules and customs
differ widely. Cousin marriage is forbidden or dep-
recated in many countries, yet in parts of Australia,
Oceania, Africa, and Asia it is regarded as the most de-
sirable form of marital union. There is no conclusive
evidence that such people are physically or mentally in-
ferior to those who avoid cousin marriage.

There is abundant evidence that the Pharaohs of
Ancient Egypt married their sisters or half sisters, and
the Ptolemies followed this precedent. The desire to
preserve the purity of the royal blood doubtless was the
chief reason for these unions. Levirate marriage, or union
with a near relative of a deceased spouse, was common in
Assyria. Herodotus and other Greek writers state that
the ancient Persians married blood relatives in the first
degree. The Greeks condemned marriage of near relatives, although it is not definitely established that the
prohibition included cousins.

Tradition ascribes to Tullius Hostilius a law that required that the guilt of incest be expiated by a sacrifice
offered by the pontiffs in the grove of Diana. Marriage
of first cousins was forbidden in the early Republic but
became quite common after the Punic Wars. Imperial
legislation on the subject of incestuous marriage was in-
timately associated with the development of the canon
law.

CHAPTER I

THE IMPEDIMENT OF CONSANGUINITY

IMPEDIMENTS to marriage, arising from the relationship of the contracting parties within stipulated limits, are of four categories. First, there is the impediment of consanguinity, which means that blood relationship exists between the parties.[1] Secondly, there is the impediment of affinity, or the relationship engendered by carnal intercourse, which brings the relatives of each party, within prescribed degrees, into the kindred of the other.[2] The third type of impediment is that known as "public honesty," wherein previous betrothal prevents the relative of one of the parties to the betrothal from marrying the other party.[3] The fourth type of impediment is that of spiritual relationship, wherein the rela-

---

[1] Gratianus, *Decretum*, in *Corpus Juris Canonici* (ed. Friedberg), Causa XXXV, Q. I; Jona Aurelianensis, *De Institutione Laicali*, in J. P. Migne (ed.), *Patrologiae Cursus Completus Series Latina* (Paris, 1844–1855), CVI, 183; Stephanus Tornacensis, *Summa* (ed. Schulte), 247; Bernardus Papiensis, *Summa* (ed. Laspeyres), 295; Petrus Lombardus, *Libri Quatuorum Sententiarum*, in Migne, *P.L.*, CXCII, 937. For modern definitions, see H. Feije, *De Impedimentis et Dispensationibus Matrimonialibus* (Louvain, 1885), Chap. XIII; M. Leitner, *Lehrbuch des katholischen Eherechts* (Paderborn, 1912), 200–28.

[2] Gratianus, *Decretum*, Causa XXXV, Q. V, X; Magister Rolandus, *Summa* (ed. Thaner), 203; Stephanus Tornacensis, *Summa*, 250; Bernardus Papiensis, *Summa*, 168; Feije, *De Impedimentis*, Chap. XIV.

[3] Gratianus, *Decretum*, Causa XXVII, Q. II; Bernardus Papiensis, *Summa*, 168; Feije, *De Impedimentis*, Chap. XV.

5

tionship emanates from joint participation in the ceremonies of baptism or confirmation.[4] Adoption has the
same effect in precluding marriage as does kinship by
blood.[5]

The legislation of the Church forbidding marriage
between blood relatives doubtless was largely influenced
by the Roman law. Plutarch narrated that "men did not
marry their kinswomen in ancient times, just as today
they do not marry their sisters or aunts." [6] Tacitus, writing of the marriage of the Emperor Claudius to Agrippina, said in part, "In the consulship of C. Pompeius
and Q. Veranus, the agreement of marriage between
Claudius and Agrippina, first concluded by rumor, then
was confirmed by illicit love; but they did not dare to
celebrate the ceremonies of marriage, since by no precedent were girls led into the home of their father's
brother." [7] Although the law prohibited marriage to a
niece, Vitellius succeeded in gaining the assent of the
Senate to the marriage on the ground that public mis-
fortune would ensue in the event that the couple were
separated. The administrative difficulties under which
the emperor labored were emphasized, and it was alleged
that the marriage would facilitate their solution.[8]

The penalty for violation of the law normally was the

---

[4] Gratianus, *Decretum*, Causa XXX, Q. I–IV; Magister Rolandus,
Summa, 144–45; Stephanus Tornacensis, *Summa*, 241; Feije, *De Impedimentis*, Chap. XVI.

[5] Ivo Carnotensis, *Decretum*, in Migne, *P.L.*, CLXI, 657.

[6] Plutarchus, *Quaestiones Romanae*, VI.

[7] Tacitus, *Annales*, XII, c. 5.

[8] *Ibid.* The law also forbade unions between an ascendant and descendant. Gaius, *Institutiones*, I, 59. In the early Republic marriage of col-
laterals was forbidden to the sixth degree. After the Punic Wars, however,
even cousin marriage became common. P. E. Corbett, *The Roman Law
of Marriage* (Oxford, 1930), 48.

nullity of the marriage so contracted and the illegitimacy of offspring born of the incestuous union.[9] The abolition of the prohibition of marriage with a niece thus would not be applicable in the event that the niece was the daughter of a sister. It is to be assumed that, in addition to the impediments mentioned by the historian and jurist, marriages among those even more closely related would be forbidden.

It was decreed during the reign of Diocletian that "no one is allowed to contract marriage with his daughter, granddaughter, or great-granddaughter; or with his aunt, sister, or daughter of his sister." [10] During the reign of the sons of Constantine, the legalization of marriage with the daughter of a brother was repealed. It was ordained that "if anyone abominably shall take as his wife the daughter of a brother or sister, or shall roll about in their embraces, he shall be bound by the pain of the capital sentence." [11] St. Ambrose rightly stated that "the Emperor Theodosius, indeed, forbade cousins to associate in the name of marriage and ordained a most severe punishment." [12]

The extension of the prohibition to include cousins was withdrawn by Arcadius, whose edict provided that such marriages should be legal, and children should be legitimate.[13] Arcadius also decreed that marriages with a sister, niece, or daughter-in-law were illegal. Anyone who contracted a forbidden marriage was permitted to

---

[9] Gaius, *Institutiones*, I, 62.

[10] *Codex Justinianus*, Lib. V, Tit. IV, c. 18.

[11] *Codex Theodosianus*, Lib. III, Tit. XII, c. 1.

[12] *Epistolae Sancti Ambrosii*, in Migne, *P.L.*, XCI, 1185; *Codex Theodosianus*, Lib. III, Tit. X, c. 1.

[13] *Codex Justinianus*, Lib. V, Tit. IV, c. 19.

retain his legal faculties during his lifetime, but his children were considered illegitimate. Any dower which the *de facto* wife brought with her reverted to the state.[14] Justinian debarred children born of an incestuous marriage from succession and, in addition, ordered the dissolution of the union and the maintenance of continence by the offenders.[15]

The passages in the Scriptures relating to the marriages of blood relatives are somewhat inconsistent. In Leviticus marriage is forbidden with father, mother, stepmother, sister, granddaughter, stepsister, aunt, and uncle.[16] On the other hand, there are passages wherein the marriage of blood relatives is condoned or even expressly enjoined. Abraham took the daughter of his brother to wife, and Isaac married Rebecca, who was related to him.[17] In Numbers, Moses in the name of the Lord commands the Children of Israel that "only to the family of the tribe of their father shall they marry." [18]

St. Augustine, in dealing with the matter, declared that since all mankind descended from Adam and Eve, marriage among brothers and sisters originally was necessary for the propagation of the race. However, "just as the compellent necessity has long ago passed, it was afterwards made damnable by religion prohibiting it." The chief reason for abstinence from consanguineous marriages allegedly was that the bonds of charity were multiplied and more widely disseminated by marriage of nonrelatives. That is, if one married his sister, his

---

[14] *Codex Theodosianus*, Lib. III, Tit. XII, c. 3.
[15] *Novellae*, Coll. II, Tit. VII, Nov. XII.
[16] XVIII, 7–14.   [17] Genesis, XI, XXIV.   [18] XXXVI, 6.

mother and his mother-in-law would be the same person; whereas, if he married a nonrelative, he would have
a mother and a mother-in-law, thus increasing the ties
of love and charity. To quote Augustine, "copulation of
man and woman, just as it adds to the mortal race, is
a nursery of charity." The Church Father was also fa-
miliar with some of the alleged physical effects of consanguineous marriage since he declared that "we learn
by experience that offspring cannot be begotten from such
a marriage." [19] St. Ambrose, in dealing with the problem, held that the marriages of blood relatives "if not
forbidden by Mosaic Law are prohibited by the law of
nature." [20]

Legislation of Synods and Councils

The so-called "Apostolic Canons" forbade marriage
with the daughter of a brother and declared that such
marriage would render the guilty man incapable of receiving clerical orders.[21] In Irish synods held under the
guidance of St. Patrick, marriages in the first four
grades of relationship were forbidden without specifica-
tion of the relations comprehended within the prohibition.[22] In the Synod of Agde, held in 506, incestuous
marriages were forbidden, again without enumeration
of the relatives thus precluded from contracting marital

[19] Augustinus, *De Civitate Dei*, XV, xvi, c. 1, in *Corpus Scriptorum
Ecclesiasticorum Latinorum* (Vienna, 1866–), XII, v, c. 2. See H. Preisker, *Christentum und Ehe in den ersten drei Jahrhunderte* (Berlin, 1921),
186.
[20] *Epistolae Sancti Ambrosii*, in Migne, *P.L.*, XCI, 1185.
[21] C. J. von Hefele, *Conciliengeschichte* (Freiburg, 1873), I, 806.
[22] *Ibid.*, II, 587.

unions.[23] The Synod of Epaon in the year 517 ordained that "besides incests which it would be shameful to name, if anyone be joined . . . with his first cousin, it is incest. Such unions are henceforth forbidden, although we do not dissolve those earlier contracted." [24] If any persons were separated for subsequently marrying in contravention to the legislation of the synod, they were to be permitted to contract new alliances.[25] In a canon of the Council of Ilerda, of doubtful authenticity, it was ordained that "concerning those who stain themselves by the pollution of incest, it is our pleasure . . . that they be admitted to mass in the church as catechumens, since, indeed, it is not allowed them to receive the food and drink of Christians as the Apostle ordered." [26]

The Second Synod of Toledo, held in 527 or 531, took action "lest a Christian desire a relative of his blood to be joined to him in marriage, although he recognizes the lines of relationship in the succession of the descent." Anyone who perpetrated the sin of incest was to be "cut off from the Body of Christ and the fellowship of the brotherhood for as many years time of excommunication as he was polluted by the stain of the blood of his kin." [27]

The Synod of Clermont of 535 forbade marriage with a cousin and decreed that "if anyone sacrilegiously disregards the authority of divine law and the laws of nature to which he ought to extend the solace of charity and a pious attitude . . . the sentence of the apostolic

---

[23] *Ibid.*, 659.   [24] *Ibid.*, 685.   [25] *Ibid.*

[26] Gratianus, *Decretum*, Causa XXXV, Q. II, III, c. 9.

[27] J. D. Mansi (ed.), *Sacrorum Conciliorum nova et amplissima Collectio* (Florence, Venice, 1759–1798), VIII, 786–87; Hefele, *Conciliengeschichte*, II, 722.

constitution is to be invoked. And as long as he goes
about in this iniquity, he will be deprived of the Christian fellowship and society as well as the communion of
Mother Church." [28]

Incestuous marriages were prohibited in general terms
by the Third Synod of Orléans held in the year 538.
Such marriages were to be strictly avoided in the future since they were really a species of adultery, and
bishops were exhorted to be more zealous in enforcing
the law. A concession, however, was made to neophytes
who, immediately subsequent to their baptism, married
relatives in ignorance of the prohibition of the Church.[29]

Earlier prohibitions were reviewed and confirmed by
the Fourth Synod of Orléans, which threatened ecclesiastical penalties against those who henceforth violated
the laws.[30] The Synod of Toul, the acts of which are
no longer extant, dealt with the question of incest.
Measures were taken in support of Archbishop Nicetus
of Rheims, who was persecuted by Frankish nobles
whom he had excommunicated for contracting illegal
marriages.[31]

The Synod of Paris in 557 forbade marriage with an
aunt on pain of ecclesiastical censure.[32] In the Trullan
Synod of 692 incestuous marriages were forbidden,
with the punishment of seven years of excommunication threatened against transgressors of the law.[33] The
Roman Synod of 743, deliberating under the supervi-

---

[28] Mansi, *Sacrorum Conciliorum Collectio*, VIII, 861; Hefele, *Conciliengeschichte*, II, 762.

[29] Mansi, *Sacrorum Conciliorum Collectio*, IX, 14; Hefele, *Conciliengeschichte*, II, 776.

[30] Hefele, *Conciliengeschichte*, II, 782.

[31] *Ibid.*, III, 6.   [32] *Ibid.*, 12–13.   [33] *Ibid.*, 337.

sion of Pope Zacharias, ordered all to refrain from marriage with cousins, nieces, and others of their kin.[34] Perpetrators of the sin of incest were to be excommunicated and anathematized, but if they relinquished the mate denied to them by the canons and performed adequate penance they could be reinstated to the Christian communion.[35] Marriages with nieces, cousins, or others of kin were condemned under pain of anathema by the Roman Synod, which met sometime between the years of 721 and 724.[36] In 745 the Council of Lessines extended the prohibitions of incestuous marriages to Christian slaves.[37]

Several interesting canons dealing with consanguinity were passed by the Synod of Compiègne (756 or 758). The assembled clergy decided that marriages of those related within the fourth degree were not to be dissolved, but if the relationship was of the third degree the marriages were to be nullified.[38] It was also decreed that if relatives in the third degree were married and one of the parties to the illicit union died, the surviving party was precluded from contracting another marriage.[39] King Pepin also threatened secular punishments against those who flouted the acts of the synod.[40] General condemnation of incestuous marriages was promulgated by the reforming synods of Riesbach, Freisingen, and Salzburg, which met during 799–800.[41]

In the ninth century there were a considerable number of synodal and conciliar enactments in regard to the marriage of blood relatives. The Synod of Aachen in

---

[34] *Ibid.*, 516–17.   [35] *Ibid.*   [36] *Ibid.*, 362.
[37] *Ibid.*, 503.   [38] *Ibid.*, 593.   [39] *Ibid.*
[40] *Monumenta Germaniae Historica, Leges,* I, 30–31.
[41] Hefele, *Conciliengeschichte,* III, 730.

802 directed all the clergy to apply themselves diligently to the dissolution and prohibition of incestuous
unions.[42] The synodal enactments were issued as a ca-
pitulary by Charlemagne.[43] The Synod of Tours in 813
ordered that all who were living in incestuous unions be
excommunicated if they did not amend their conduct.[44]
In the Roman Synod, convoked in 826 by Pope Eugenius II (824–827), marriages of kindred were forbidden, with cousins and nieces specifically mentioned.
Violators of the law were to be excommunicated until
they dissolved their illicit unions and proved amenable
to penitential measures applied at the discretion of the
local priests.[45] The reform Synod of Paris, held in 829,
enumerated incest as one of the many evils which were
afflicting the Church, and the clergy were admonished
strictly to enforce the canons forbidding such unions.[46]
The prelates and lower clergy, assembled at Mainz in
847, declared that "we forbid that anyone be married in
the fourth generation: where indeed this is found to
have been done after this prohibition, [the union] is
to be dissolved." [47] The Synod of Worms enacted that
whoever had entered upon an illegal marriage, "if he
will perform adequate penance and is not able to maintain continence, it is allowed him to take a legitimate
woman in marriage. Similarly, a woman who has lapsed
into that iniquity shall do likewise in order that she be
not lost in the chaos of fornication." [48]

[42] Mansi, *Sacrorum Conciliorum Collectio*, XIV, App., 257; Hefele,
Conciliengeschichte, III, 743.
[43] *M.G.H.*, Leg., I, 91.   [44] Hefele, *Conciliengeschichte*, III, 763.
[45] *Ibid.*, IV, 50.   [46] *Ibid.*, 67.   [47] *Ibid.*, 128.
[48] Mansi, *Sacrorum Conciliorum Collectio*, XV, 875; Hefele, *Conciliengeschichte*, IV, 371.

The Synod of Douci (Douzy), held in 874, promulgated a plaintive canon attempting to put an end to illegal marriages. The clergy therein assembled pointed out that "it is to our humiliation that it was reported by no uncertain relation and consultation how many go to ruin in deadly pestilence in incestuous marriages, especially the nobles by blood and those exalted in temporal honor." [49] Even though, as had been alleged, Gregory I (590–604) permitted the English to marry their relatives in the fourth degree, and even in the third, the synod declared that the transgressions of the English had been condoned because of their ignorance of the law and the pope's reluctance to discourage the new converts by premature rigor. Christians were admonished to refrain from marriage to the seventh degree despite the allegations of "teachers of errors who refused to be disciples of truth." In substantiation of their contentions the synod declared that the Roman law had debarred children begotten from the marriage of relatives to the seventh degree from succession to an estate.[50]

In 909 the Synod of Trosle forbade the marriage of relatives and declared that, according to Roman law, no legitimate heirs could be born of an incestuous marriage.[51] In the great synod held under the direction of Henry II of Germany in the first year of his reign (1002), the assembled prelates were chided for their apathy in enforcing the law of the Church. The king was reported to have declared that "among many things

---

[49] Mansi, *Sacrorum Conciliorum Collectio*, XVII, 282; Hefele, *Conciliengeschichte*, IV, 511.
[50] Hefele, *Conciliengeschichte*, IV, 511.   [51] *Ibid.*, 574.

which are to be corrected in our kingdom and in your parishes is that relatives, very close to each other, are joined in marriage; so that, not fearing God and not revering men, they do not shrink from associating in marriage a relative even of the third degree, which is horrible to say; and they do not fear to violate the line to the seventh degree which the sacred canons order to be observed." The bishops were much embarrassed by the charge. Many of them knew that they had consciously relaxed the laws in the interest of their friends. The irate king went on to declare that "you are holding the places of holy priests and you sit in a better seat than did Moses, representing the Lord, and you ought to be called good watchdogs and holy rams for the merit of life; on the contrary, you are mute dogs not wishing to be moved to bark, and the blind lead the blind so that both fall into the ditch." [52]

Marriages of relatives up to the sixth or seventh degree were forbidden by the Synod of Bourges in 1031,[53] while in 1047 a similar assembly at Elne declared marriages of blood relatives up to the sixth degree to be incestuous.[54] The famous reform Synod of Rheims of 1049, held under the auspices of Pope Leo IX, forbade incestuous marriages in general terms.[55] The important Lateran Synod of 1059 promulgated a canon which stated that relationship up to the seventh degree precluded marriage. According to the enactment, the seventh degree was specified since relationship could not be traced beyond it.[56]

[52] Constantinus, *Vita Adalberonis*, in *M.G.H., Scriptores*, IV, 663.
[53] Mansi, *Sacrorum Conciliorum Collectio*, XIX, 505.
[54] Hefele, *Conciliengeschichte*, IV, 701.
[55] *Ibid.*, 731.   [56] *Ibid.*, 824–25.

The Synod of Vienne and Tours of 1060 enacted a canon which proscribed marriage of blood relatives, in addition to other provisions ordaining impediments to marriage arising from other circumstances.[57] In 1072 the Synod of Rouen forbade marriage of kin up to the seventh degree of relationship. Priests who wittingly married a couple related within the stipulated degrees were ordered deposed.[58]

Alexander II (1061–1073), probably in a Roman synod, decreed that consanguineous marriages could not be condoned because of gifts, prayers, and offerings made by the offending parties.[59] The Synod of Lillebonne of 1080, attended by William the Conqueror, promulgated a canon to the effect that "concerning those who hold wives of their relation and kin, the bishops shall apply canonical justice. The king [William], indeed, bears or tolerates none of this, but admonishes the bishops to judge more firmly so that the law of God be firmly kept." [60]

The Synod of Garonne, held during the pontificate of Gregory VII (1073–1086) in order to put into effect his famous reform decrees, issued a canon threatening excommunication against all who contracted illegal marriages and obdurately adhered to the illicit compacts.[61] The Council of Nîmes, held during the pontificate of Urban II (1087–1099), declared that those "who publicly take to wife relatives or adultresses are to be excomunicated as long as they retain them." [62]

[57] *Ibid.*, 841–42.   [58] *Ibid.*, 592.
[59] Mansi, *Sacrorum Conciliorum Collectio*, XIX, 979.
[60] *Ibid.*, XX, 555; Hefele, *Conciliengeschichte*, V, 155.
[61] Hefele, *Conciliengeschichte*, V, 128.
[62] Mansi, *Sacrorum Conciliorum Collectio*, XX, 933.

In the twelfth century the canons were equally numerous. The Synod of London in 1102 nullified marriages within the seventh degree and held that anyone who knew of such a union and did not lodge information with the proper ecclesiastical authorities shared the guilt of incest.[63] The Lateran Council of 1123 forbade the marriage of relatives and declared that anyone who contracted such a marriage was to be considered infamous and incapable of succeeding to an inheritance.[64] Marriage of relatives to the seventh degree was forbidden by a London synod in 1125.[65] The Synod of Clermont issued a prohibition of incest without specifying to what limits the ban was to extend.[66]

In 1166 the Eastern Church took measures against consanguineous marriages. The Synod of Constantinople, held in that year, assailed marriages of those related up to the seventh degree of kinship. In the preceding century the Patriarch Alexius had allowed marriages already contracted within the forbidden degrees to continue, but the privilege had been abused. Henceforth, the prohibition was to be absolute, and illegal marriages were to be dissolved without regard for extenuating circumstances.[67] The Emperor Manuel commended the clergy for their action and confirmed their legislation by an imperial edict.[68]

The Irish Synod of Cassel (Cashel) of 1171 outlawed the marriages of relatives in a general prohibition.[69] The Synod of Dioclea, held in 1199, declared that the law, emanating from the Roman Church, "the

---

[63] Hefele, *Conciliengeschichte*, V, 269.   [64] *Ibid.*, 380.
[65] *Ibid.*, 391.   [66] *Ibid.*, 410.   [67] *Ibid.*, 680.
[68] Mansi, *Sacrorum Conciliorum Collectio*, XXII, 22.
[69] Hefele, *Conciliengeschichte*, V, 683.

mother and teacher of all churches," voided marriages up to the seventh degree. Yet there were many in Dalmatia who "not having the fear of God, did not hesitate to contract marriages with relatives in the fourth or fifth degree or even closer, against the constitutions of the Holy Fathers." Henceforth, these transgressors were to be afflicted with the punishment of excommunication until they sundered the illicit unions and performed suitable penance.[70] The last instance of synodal or conciliar action in the matter of consanguinity prior to the assembly of the Fourth Lateran Council in 1215 was a canon of the Synod of London in 1200.[71]

PAPAL DECRETALS

There are no authentic papal decretals bearing on the subject of consanguinity as an impediment to marriage prior to the pontificate of Gregory I. This pontiff issued a decision to the effect that no one was to take to wife any of his kindred to the seventh degree of relationship and based his position on the provision of the secular law which extended the succession to an inheritance to the relatives in the seventh degree.[72]

Gregory II (715–731), writing to St. Boniface in 726, declared that "marriages of relatives are to be forbidden," but "because temperance, especially among a barbaric people, is more pleasing than the strictness of censure, it is to be conceded that they be joined after

---

[70] *Ibid.*, 795.   [71] *Ibid.*, 797.

[72] Gratianus, *Decretum*, Causa XXXV, Q. II, III, c. 1. He modified the severity of this decretal by condoning such marriages if contracted in ignorance of the prohibition of the law. *Ibid.*, Q. VIII, c. 1.

the fourth generation." [73] Zacharias (741–752), in addition to addressing letters to Frankish nobles exhorting them to observe the marital law,[74] issued important rulings in regard to affinity and spiritual relationship. Leo IV (847–855), in writing to the Anglo-Saxon bishops, answered their query by declaring that no one was permitted to marry a wife from his own kindred under pain of anathema.[75]

Nicholas I (858–867) was active in legislating in regard to impediments to marriage resulting from the relationship of the parties. In 867 he wrote that "whoever cherish marriages of relatives ought to take heed lest they fall in the gulf of the devil, since it is obvious that they devour themselves in rejecting Christ's teaching." [76] In 865 he declared that those who married their blood relatives "in the manner of beasts" were to be shunned. Illegal marriages should be dissolved, and continence be observed thereafter by the parties. If, however, one party to an illicit union died, the survivor was permitted to contract a new union if he could not be persuaded to remain continent.[77]

The legislation of Nicholas was also important since he attempted to apply a scale of penance, graduated in severity in direct relation to the proximity in kinship between the parties to an illicit marriage. If the incest

---

[73] Migne, *P.L.*, LXXXIX, 524–25. It is possible that this may mean the fifth generation. The German method of reckoning according to *genicula* did not count the relatives in the first canonical degree of relationship as a degree. J. Freisen, *Geschichte des canonischen Eherechts* (Paderborn, 1893), 411, 435.

[74] P. Jaffé (ed.), *Bibliotheca Rerum Germanicarum* (Berlin, 1869), III, 114, 121.

[75] Migne, *P.L.*, CXV, 668.   [76] *Ibid.*, CXIX, 1131.

[77] *Ibid.*, 919–20.

were committed with an aunt, cousin, grandchild, or
grandparent, or if certain degrees of affinity were disregarded, both guilty parties were liable to the following punishment: In the first year they were banned
from the Church and were to subsist on bread, water,
and salt, except on Sundays and feast days. During the
second year the restrictions on church attendance were
removed, and the penitents were allowed wine and meat
on Sundays and feast days.[78] During the third and
fourth years the repentant sinners were required to abstain from either wine or meat regularly, but on Sundays and holy days they might indulge in both. From
then on until the tenth year the penitents observed three
fasts per year and were forbidden to carry and use arms
except against pagans. During this period no new marital alliances could be contracted by the offending parties.
For those who had been in incestuous relations with
mother, sister, or daughter, the penalties were much
more severe; thus, seven years of fasting on a diet of
bread and water were prescribed, to be followed by observation of three fasts annually for twenty-one years.[79]

From the death of Nicholas to the pontificate of
Clement III, there were many papal decretals concerning
the marriage of relatives; but since they were in reference to affinity or spiritual relationship, or concerned
the mode of computing the degrees, or the procedure
by which a marriage was to be examined, they will be
discussed under separate heads.

Clement III (1187–1191) decided that marriages
contracted within the fifth degree of relationship were invalid, even though the nuptial ceremonies had been

[78] *Ibid.*, 1132–33.   [79] *Ibid.*

carried out according to the stipulated canonical procedure, and the marriage had been consummated by
carnal copulation.[80] The same pontiff ordered that
where incestuous marriages were invalidated the dowry
must be returned to the woman.[81]

Celestine III (1191–1198) heralded, to some degree,
the relaxation of the rigor of the law that was to come
during the rule of his illustrious successor, Innocent III.
He declared that where the parties were related within
the sixth degree on one side and in the fifth degree
through another line, a marriage could legitimately take
place. However, if the couple were related within the
sixth degree through one line and in the second or third
degree through another, marriage was thereby precluded.[82]

The Fourth Lateran Council marked an epoch in
the history of the impediment of consanguinity in that
the severity of the seventh degree prohibition was mitigated by allowing marriage among those related beyond
the fourth degree.[83] Canon L set forth that "the prohibition of conjugal union shall certainly not go beyond
the fourth degree of consanguinity and of affinity, since,
in the more remote grades, a prohibition of this kind
cannot be universally observed without grave damage.
Indeed, the four-fold number accords with the prohibition of carnal union of which the Apostle said that a
man does not have the power of his body but the woman
has; and the woman does not have the power of her

[80] *Decretales Gregorii IX Papae*, in *Corpus Juris Canonici*, Lib. II,
Tit. XIX, c. 6.

[81] *Ibid.*, Lib. IV, Tit. XX, c. 3.   [82] *Ibid.*, Lib. IV, Tit. XIV, c. 3.

[83] C. J. von Hefele and H. Leclerq, *Histoire des conciles* (Paris, 1907),
V, Pt. II, 1372.

body but the man, because there are four humors in the body which exist from the four elements." [84]

There were a few enactments in the period which were passed subsequent to the Lateran Council. The Synod of Bremen in 1266 bemoaned the frequency of marriage within the forbidden degrees since many "moved by the passion of their flesh or deceived by earthly cupidity do not shrink to immerse themselves in the filth of incestuous luxury and to pollute the sacrament of marriage as much as they can by contracting, within the forbidden degrees, *de facto* unions, which, it was ordained, are to be called not marriages but concubinage." All who formed such unions were to be excommunicated, and priests who connived at the infraction of the law were to be deposed.[85] The Synod of Torcello, held in 1296, took similar action.[86]

In reviewing the legislation of councils and popes forbidding marriage in various degrees of blood relationship, nothing has been said as to the way in which the degree of relationship was to be computed. This problem, however, was such a difficult one that official legislation, together with the writings of many canonists who felt called upon to explain or propound various schemes of calculation, failed for a long time to evolve a settled system. For a clear understanding of the difficulties involved, the matter requires a detailed discussion.

[84] *Ibid.*   [85] Hefele, *Conciliengeschichte*, VI, 97.
[86] *Ibid.*, 368.

Chapter II

CALCULATION OF THE DEGREE OF RELATIONSHIP

THE difficulties besetting the ecclesiastical authorities in determining degrees of relationship were rooted in the provisions of the Roman law regarding intestate succession. Paulus in his "Sentences" [1] had written that the determination of degrees of propinquity involved two lines. In the first grade in the upper, or ascending, line were embraced father and mother; in the lower, or descending, line were included son and daughter. In the second grade in the upper line were grandfather and grandmother; in the lower line were included grandson and granddaughter. The relationship thus was computed up to the seventh grade. Attention was also drawn to the fact that there were two sets of relatives; that is, those descending through the male line, called the agnates, and those descending through the female line who were called cognates. Thus, in the second grade in the ascending line there would be the paternal grandparents and the maternal grandparents; in the lower line there would be grandchildren through sons and grandchildren through daughters.

In discussing intestate succession, the same jurist, after defining intestates, declared that the inheritance

---

[1] Paulus, *Libri Quinque Sententiarum* (ed. Krüger), IV, xi.

was to go to the relatives in regular order. First came
the son and daughter, who were in the *potestas* of the
father at his death; next in order, grandson, granddaughter, great-grandson, great-granddaughter, and so
on, "descending in the masculine sex through the son,"
that is, only agnates could succeed.[2]

Justinian by his legislation effected a revolution in
the law of intestate succession. The principle of agna-
tion was practically abolished, and the succession made
entirely dependent upon blood kinship.[3] Thus, in the
second grade, for example, there would be succeeding
in order grandchildren through a son and grandchildren
through a daughter, which would in effect double the
number of grades. It was this legislation of Justinian
that caused the greatest difficulty to the canonists since,
when these provisions became known through the re-
vival of the study of the Roman law, there were many
who claimed that the same system should apply in calculating relationship for the purpose of marriage, which
was tantamount to relaxing the rigor of the ecclesiastical
law by half. Agnatal succession, together with the calculation of the degree of proximity derived by reckoning the number of generations one was removed from
the intestate, was also a feature of some of the Germanic codes.[4]

The Christian law took over the Roman system of
reckoning relationship as explained by Paulus, that is,
each generation constituted a degree. The count also
was extended up to the seventh degree as was the case
in the Roman law; but the Church applied this reckon-

[2] *Ibid.*   [3] *Novellae*, Nov. CXXVII.
[4] *Edictus Rothari*, in *M.G.H., Leg.*, IV, c. 153.

ing to the seventh degree in the prohibition of marriage, which, of course, was a much more rigorous prohibition than found in the Roman laws of incest.

The first attempt by a canonist to establish a system to determine the degree of relationship was made by Isidore of Seville, who held that the son and daughter were to constitute the trunk, and the grandson and granddaughter were to be the first branch or degree; that is, they were one generation removed from the trunk.[5] Rabanus Maurus set forth that the Roman law permitted marriage between first cousins, but that the Christian law forbade this because "offspring cannot be begotten from such a union." He also held that marriage could be permitted in the third or fourth degree but not in the second. He went on to state that if any wished to remain continent to the fifth, sixth, or even seventh degree they were not to be prevented from doing so, because "the farther one is removed by separation, the farther one is from destruction." He failed to state, however, just how the degree of propinquity was to be determined.[6]

Benedictus Levita held that no Christian was to take a wife from his kindred to the seventh generation. While he did not state explicitly that a generation was to be equivalent to a degree, that seems to have been his position.[7]

---

[5] Isidorus, *Etymologiae* (ed. Lindsay), Lib. IX, c. 3.

[6] Rabanus Maurus, *Tractatus de Consanguineorum Nuptiis*, in Migne, *P.L.*, CX, 1093. "Third or fourth degree" may mean fourth and fifth if the Germanic method of computation was employed. Freisen, *Geschichte des canonischen Eherechts*, 411.

[7] Benedictus Levita, *Capitularium*, in *M.G.H.*, *Leg.*, II, 2, c. 130, 432, 435.

Burchard of Worms quoted Isidore to the effect that relationship extended to the sixth degree. The son and daughter were to constitute the trunk, with the grandson and granddaughter in the first degree. There were six degrees to represent the six ages of the world.[8] In chapter twenty-eight, in a fuller exposition of the degrees of kinship, his scheme is essentially that of the Roman jurist Paulus. He held that there were two lines, the ascendant and the descendent, with the collateral lines beginning in the second degree. In the first grade in the ascendant line were the father and mother; in the second grade in the ascendant line were the grandfather and grandmother; in the descendent line were grandson and granddaughter. He took no cognizance of a differentiation between agnates and cognates but considered them in the same degree. Thus, a grandson through a son and a grandson through a daughter would be in the second degree since both were two generations removed from a common ancestor.[9]

The Synod of Douci, held in 874, took the same position in regard to counting the degrees of relationship and declared that the Roman law debarred children begotten of marriages of relatives up to the seventh degree from succession to an inheritance.[10] Here is the confused idea of the Roman law which is to be found reiterated in subsequent canonical treatises. That is, the Roman law did count relationship up to and including the sixth degree for the purpose of determining the succession to an intestate inheritance, but it did not in

---

[8] Burchardus Wormaiensis, *Decretum*, in Migne, *P.L.*, CXL, 781.
[9] *Ibid.*, 784.
[10] Mansi, *Sacrorum Conciliorum Collectio*, XVII, 282.

any way prohibit marriage contracted within degrees of relationship more remote than first cousins. The canonists, however, erroneously combined the Roman law of intestate succession with the provisions in respect to incest and fallaciously asserted that the Romans had barred marriages up to the seventh degree of blood relationship.

John of Orléans gave the essence of a popular theory as to the reason for the extension of the prohibition to the seventh degree. He declared that there were to be no marriages among those related up to the seventh degree of kinship since relationship by blood could not be traced beyond that point, there being no names available for relatives more distant than the sixth degree.[11] Thus the provision "up to the seventh degree" did not include the seventh degree since the relationship could not be traced beyond the sixth. Beyond the sixth degree the ties of kinship were conceived as being, in a sense, dissipated, to be gathered up again by marriage, whereupon the cycle was repeated.

The Synod of Seligenstadt, held in 1022, promulgated a canon which clearly indicated that the method of computation was by no means fixed. It was decreed that "there are some who wish to count the generations of consanguinity so that brother and sister are in the first degree. However, the holy synod ordains that, just as it is decreed by the ancient fathers, nephew and niece, that is, son of a brother and daughter of a sister, are considered to be in the first degree."[12]

[11] Jona Aurelianensis, *De Institutione Laicali*, in Migne, *P.L.*, CVI, 183–84.
[12] Mansi, *Sacrorum Conciliorum Collectio*, XIX, 398; Hefele, *Conciliengeschichte*, IV, 673.

The decretals of Pope Alexander II were of great importance in establishing the canonical system of reckoning relationship. In 1063 he wrote to the bishops, clergy, and judges of Italy informing them that "in a synod held in the consistory of the Lateran, action was taken concerning the new and unheard of error of those who, affirming that natural brothers or sisters between themselves are in the second degree, and their sons or daughters in the fourth, and their grandsons and granddaughters in the sixth degree, say that these men and women can contract marriage among themselves by law." [13] Whence did these disseminators of false doctrine derive justification for their position? They were quoting the Roman law and "to this profane error they advanced in argument the laws which the Emperor Justinian promulgated concerning the succession of relatives." But, as the pope pointed out, the Roman laws on this point were framed for a different purpose than were the church laws. The Roman laws were devised to determine the order of succession to an estate, whereas the canonical computation was concerned with marriage. If one were to apply the Roman laws of succession as amended by Justinian, who abolished the provisions in favor of agnates, he would have to count two degrees for each generation; that is, one for the agnate and one for the cognate. In the second generation, then, there would be the grandchildren through a son and grandchildren through a daughter, and each group would be counted a degree, making two degrees to a generation. Applied to the church laws of marriage, this method of calculation would have the effect of con-

[13] Migne, *P.L.*, CXLVI, 1379.

tracting by half the severity of the canonical prohibitions of marriage among relatives. Alexander pointed out that the system was all very well for application to inheritances, but since marriage involved two persons, it was eminently fitting that in the canon law two persons should constitute one degree.[14]

In his well-known answers to the Neapolitan clergy, Alexander II combated another error that had arisen concerning the determination of the degrees of relationship of descendants of two or more brothers. The pontiff learned that the clergy of Naples were troubled by "the difficulty of the famous question," since "pernicious expositors and disputants, sitting indeed in the seat of pestilence, speak laws of which they are ignorant and teach that which they on no account establish." These propagators of error asserted that grandsons who were sons of two brothers were in the fourth degree.[15] The pope quoted scripture to demolish the arguments of his opponents. In Genesis it is stated that "Joseph lived an hundred and ten years" [16] and further that "Joseph saw Ephraim's children of the third generation." [17] But, as the pope pointed out, Ephra and Manasseh also had sons who were grandsons of Joseph, so that if the contentions of his antagonists were correct, the passage in the Bible should read "children of the sixth generation." [18]

The controversy continued. Ivo of Chartres in his *Decretum* accepted essentially the position of Alexander II and quoted the dictum of Isidore to the effect that the son and daughter constituted the trunk, with

---

[14] *Ibid.*, 1381–83.   [15] *Ibid.*, 1402.   [16] L, 22.
[17] L, 23.   [18] Migne, *P.L.*, CXLVI, 1379.

the grandson and the granddaughter making up the first degree.[19] In Ivo's treatment of specific cases we obtain more information as to the mode of calculation he employed. In the case of King Henry I of England, who wished to marry his daughter to a son of Hugh of Gervais, he traced the descent of the parties back to two sisters from whom they were six generations removed. He clearly computed the degree of relationship by counting the number of generations the parties were mutually removed from a common ancestor, in this case the father of two sisters; and finding the prospective married couple related within the sixth degree, he forbade them to marry.[20] In other cases that came within his competence, he also utilized this mode of computation.[21]

Peter Damiani attacked the contention, which was apparently still current, to the effect that grandsons through two brothers were related, not in the second, but in the fourth degree. He repeated the arguments of Alexander II based on the passages of Genesis. He inveighed against the practice in vogue in some quarters of counting two degrees to the generation, that is, one for the agnate and one for the cognate.[22] He based his argument on a spurious bull of Gregory the Great, wherein permission was conceded to the Anglo-Saxons to contract marriages with relatives beyond the fourth degree.[23] If the system of calculation of two degrees to

[19] Ivo Carnotensis, *Decretum*, in Migne, *P.L.*, CLXI, 658 ff.
[20] *Epistolae Ivonis Carnotensis*, in Migne, *P.L.*, CLXII, 163–64.
[21] *Ibid.*, 139-40, 255-56.
[22] Petrus Damianus, *De Parentelae Gradibus*, in Migne, *P.L.*, CXLV, 196 ff.
[23] Migne, *P.L.*, LXXVII, 1320–22; *Decretales Pseudo-Isidorianae et Capitula Angilramni* (ed. Hinschius), 749.

a generation were correct, he held that the relaxation conceded by Gregory was tantamount to permission for the son of one brother to marry the daughter of another, which would be "insane" since the same pontiff had expressly forbidden the marriage of cousins.[24]

Gratian cited the system of Isidore [25] and the letters of Alexander II.[26] In regard to the position of brothers, he cited Pope Zacharias to the effect that "I and my brother are one generation and we make the first degree, and we are distant in no grade from one another. Likewise, my son and the son of my brother are in the second degree," and so on up to and including the sixth degree.[27]

Cardinal Roland, later to become the famous Pope Alexander III (1159–1181), held that a number of sons constituted one grade, just as *amo, amas, amat* were not three words but three parts of the same word. He also cited the Trinity as an example wherein three persons constituted one essence. The system that had been proposed, wherein the sons of two brothers were in the fourth degree, the sons of three brothers in the sixth, and so on, had been repudiated by the canonists. However, there still remained considerable divergence in interpretation, for Roland declared that some considered the original couple the first degree.[28]

Peter Lombard added nothing to the clarification of the law. He, too, cited Isidore of Seville and explained his mode of determining relationship, asserting that the

---

[24] Petrus Damianus, *De Parentelae Gradibus*, in Migne, *P.L.*, CXLV, 196 ff.

[25] Gratianus, *Decretum*, Causa XXXV, Q. V, c. 1.

[26] *Ibid.*, c. 2–3.   [27] *Ibid.*, c. 4.

[28] Magister Rolandus, *Summa*, 202.

six degrees were adopted to signify the six ages of the world.[29] He also stated that kinship was dissipated after the sixth degree, but marriage gathered up the scattered threads, and the cycle began anew. He held that where marriage was forbidden to the sixth degree, it was intended that the calculation should begin with the sons and daughters, who were to be considered as constituting the first degree, with the grandchildren making up the second degree, and so on up to and including the sixth degree.[30]

The *Summa* of Stephen of Tournai furnished a fairly finished presentation of the law governing the calculation of the degree of kinship. He pointed out that there were two modes of counting relationship, that is, the canonical and the legal.[31] Two persons constituted a canonical grade, whereas one person could constitute a legal grade. The difference in the modes of computation arose from the fact that "in the laws, grades are determined so that the inheritance be allocated to certain persons legitimately, i. e., so that whoever is closer in either *agnatio* or *cognatio* be called to the succession. The inheritance, indeed, can be suitable to one person, nor is it absurd, if, for this reason, that one person constitutes a grade. In the canon law, however, it is suitable that grades be found distinct so that it may be shown what persons can be joined legally in marriage and to what persons it is forbidden. Marriages, indeed, cannot exist unless between two persons. It is necessary, there-

---

[29] Petrus Lombardus, *Libri Quatuorum Sententiarum*, in Migne, *P.L.*, CXCII, 937.

[30] *Ibid.*   [31] Stephanus Tornacensis, *Summa*, 247–48.

fore, according to the canons, that two persons be made one canonical grade." [32]

Apparently, there was still some divergence in the mode of beginning the reckoning since Stephen held that "the counting begins with the brothers according to some and with the sons of the brothers according to others." He gave a clear definition of what was meant by the term "grade." He declared that "they are in the same grade . . . who are equally distant from the *stirps*, that is, the person from whom they descend, as two brothers, two sons from the same father, the sons of two brothers, the daughters of two brothers, or the son and daughter of two brothers." [33]

There was as yet one question left unanswered. In what degree of relationship were those who were unequally removed from a common ancestor? Bernard of Pavia first clearly expressed the doctrine that was to be followed. He stated that "it is to be noted that if any descend unequally from the ancestor, that is to say, one descends in the fourth, fifth, or sixth degree and the other in the seventh degree, they are distant from one another in the seventh degree." [34] That is, where the lines of descent from a common ancestor were unequal, the longer line was to be considered the determinative factor. Thus if a woman were five degrees removed from the common ancestor, and a man were eight degrees removed, the parties would be considered to be in the eighth degree to each other and would be eligible for legal marriage.

[32] *Ibid.*, 254–55.   [33] *Ibid.*, 255.
[34] Bernardus Papiensis, *Summa*, 167–68.

This rule was formally incorporated into the canon law by a decretal of Gregory IX (1227–1241), which declared that where a man and a woman who desired to marry were related to a common ancestor in different degrees the longer line was to be the determining factor in calculating the degree of relationship between them.[35]

By about 1280 the law was rounded out, and John de Deo in his "Tree of Consanguinity" stated the complete scheme. The degree was the number of generations between the parties and the common ancestor, excluding the common ancestor who was not counted as a degree. In the event that the lines were unequal, the longer line was to be taken as determining the degree.[36] These calculations, of course, were carried out only up to and including the fourth degree since the Fourth Lateran Council had abolished the restrictions on marriage in a degree of relationship farther removed.

[35] *Decretales Gregorii IX Papae*, Lib. IV, Tit. XIV, c. 9.
[36] John de Deo, *Declaratio Arboris Consanguinitatis*, in *Corpus Juris Canonici*, I, 1433–36.

CHAPTER III

THE IMPEDIMENT OF AFFINITY

CHRISTIAN legislation dealing with affinity also was preceded by enactments of the Roman law, which doubtless influenced the course of the legislation of the early Church. Gaius said that marriage to a mother-in-law, daughter-in-law, or stepdaughter was illegal and subject to the same disabilities as applied to incestuous unions where the relationship of the parties was one of blood.[1]

A law issued in the name of Valentinian and Theodosius declared that "we remove the liberty for taking to wife the wife of a brother and for the contracting to two sisters."[2] Theodosius and his son Honorius ordained that "It is considered that he will commit incest who, after the loss of a first wife, shall believe that her sister may be chosen in marriage. For equal and similar reason, if anyone believes that marriages are to be sought after the death of a mate from among her relatives, it follows without a doubt that from this union legitimate children will not result, nor shall they receive the paternal inheritance."[3]

Arcadius, in forbidding incestuous marriages with

---

[1] Gaius, *Institutiones*, I, 62.
[2] *Codex Theodosianus*, Lib. III, Tit. XII, c. 2; *Codex Justinianus*, Lib. V, Tit. V, c. 5.
[3] *Codex Theodosianus*, Lib. III, Tit. XII, c. 4.

kindred, included the daughter-in-law in his enumeration of those with whom legitimate marriage could not be contracted.[4] The Emperor Zeno prohibited marriage to the widow of a deceased brother, even if it were alleged that the woman had retained her virginity while joined to the brother.[5] Anastasius also issued an edict strictly prohibiting union with the widow of a deceased brother.[6]

In the *Digest*, Modestinus was quoted to the effect that "affines are relatives of a man's wife so called because two kinships, which are different from each other, are joined in marriage, and the one assumes the limits of the kinship of the other." He also enumerated all the relatives that were comprehended within the category of affines and defined each, but he held the affinity to be nullified if it emanated from a marriage illegitimately contracted.[7]

The biblical injunctions against marriage with affines are found mainly in Leviticus, where marriage is forbidden with stepmother or stepsister, or with daughter-in-law or sister-in-law.[8] In the same chapter intercourse is forbidden with near relatives of a woman with whom carnal relations had been enjoyed.[9] The penalty for transgression of these provisions was ostracism from the Chosen People as well as punishment for the souls of offenders.[10]

---

[4] *Ibid.*, c. 3.   [5] *Codex Justinianus*, Lib. V, Tit. V, c. 8.
[6] *Ibid.*, c. 9.   [7] *Digesta Justiniana*, Lib. XXXVIII, Tit. X, c. 4.
[8] XVIII, 11.   [9] *Ibid.*, 15, 16.   [10] *Ibid.*, 29.

Legislation of Synods and Councils

A large number of enactments by synods and councils forbade marriage with relatives through marriage or carnal intercourse. The Synod of Elvira in 306 decreed that "if anyone, after the death of his wife, shall take her sister to wife, and she be a Christian, it seems good that he abstain five years from communion unless the necessity of sickness compels absolution to be granted sooner." [11] The same synod ordered that those who married daughters-in-law were to be deprived of communion until death was imminent.[12]

In the Synod of Ancyra, held in 314, a particular case was discussed. A married man rendered the sister of his wife pregnant, and the latter hanged herself because of the disgrace. The resultant scandal was so serious that it brought the matter within the cognizance of the synod. It was ordained that all who were in any wise implicated were to do penance for ten years before they could be received in the fourth grade of penitents.[13]

The Synod of New Caesarea, sometime between the years 314 and 325, ordered that "if a woman marries [successively] two brothers, she shall be excommunicated until in danger of death; however, for the sake of mercy, she shall become eligible to penance if she

[11] Mansi, *Sacrorum Conciliorum Collectio*, II, 15; Hefele, *Conciliengeschichte*, I, 183.

[12] Hefele, *Conciliengeschichte*, I, 185.

[13] *Ibid.*, 242. The Council of Trent in 1563 decreed that affinity engendered by illicit intercourse was not to enforce separation beyond the second degree. Leitner, *Lehrbuch des katholischen Eherechts*, 218–19. The guilty party, however, may forfeit his conjugal rights. P. J. Brillaud, *Traité pratique des empêchements et des dispenses de mariage* (Paris, 1871), 14.

promises to sunder that forbidden union. If, however, the woman or the man shall die in that union, then the penance for the surviving party shall be severe."[14]

In 402 the Roman Synod, held under the direction of Innocent I (402–417), forbade the marriage of any Christian with the sister of a deceased wife.[15] The Synod of Agde in 506 promulgated a canon relegating to the rank of catechumens those who contracted marriage with the widow of a brother, with the sister of a deceased wife, with a mother-in-law, or with a daughter-in-law.[16]

Marriage with the widow of a brother, as well as with the sister of a deceased wife, was forbidden by the Council of Orléans in 511.[17] In 517 the Synod of Epaon decreed that marriages with stepmothers, widows of brothers, sisters-in-law, or aunts by marriage were to be eschewed since they were incestuous.[18] The Second Synod of Orléans ordained in 533 that no one could marry a stepmother.[19] The Synod of Clermont of 535 invoked excommunication against those who contracted incestuous alliances with the widow of a brother, with sister-in-law, daughter-in-law, or aunt by marriage.[20] The Synod of Paris in 557 outlawed marriages with a widowed sister-in-law, stepmother, aunt by marriage, niece by marriage, and stepdaughter.[21]

During the eighth century a considerable group of canons were issued confirming or extending disabilities for marriages among affines. The Roman Synod of 743 specifically mentioned stepmother and wife of a de-

---

[14] Hefele, *Conciliengeschichte*, I, 244.   [15] *Ibid.*, II, 88.
[16] *Ibid.*, 659.   [17] *Ibid.*, 664.   [18] *Ibid.*, 685.
[19] *Ibid.*, 757.   [20] *Ibid.*, 762.   [21] *Ibid.*, III, 12–13.

ceased brother as those with whom marriage was not to be contracted, although it is quite possible that the enumeration was not designed to be exclusive.[22]

The Synod of Vermeria (Verberie), held in the year 753, declared that if anyone transgressed with his stepdaughter he was to separate both from his wife and from the woman with whom he had the illicit relations.[23] Both parties to the sinful connection were to eschew marriage permanently, but the innocent wife was to be permitted to remarry provided she had abstained from carnal intercourse with her husband as soon as she learned of his derelictions with her daughter.[24] The same synod issued a canon prohibiting the practice of sleeping with a stepdaughter or sister-in-law.[25]

A ruling adopted by the Synod of Compiègne, held in 757 or 758, stated that if anyone had carnal relations with a woman and her daughter and subsequently married another woman, his marriage was to be dissolved. The women with whom he carried on his illicit affairs, however, were to be allowed to contract legitimate marriages if each were ignorant of her paramour's relations with the other. It was also ordained that anyone who had intercourse with two sisters was to be debarred from marriage, but the women with whom he sinned were eligible for marriage if they were ignorant of the fact that he was in carnal relations with both.[26]

The Synod of Rome in 826 included stepmother and widow of a brother among those with whom marriage

[22] *Ibid.*, 516.   [23] *Ibid.*, 574.
[24] *Ibid.* The text in *M.G.H.*, *Leg.*, I, 22, adds "if she cannot remain continent."
[25] Hefele, *Conciliengeschichte*, III, 574.   [26] *Ibid.*, 595.

was to be avoided on pain of anathema.[27] The Synod of
Worms in 868 included those who had sinned with two
sisters among those who would be permitted to contract legitimate unions if they performed adequate penance for their sin.[28] The Synod of Tribur, held twenty-
seven years later, was more severe. The assembled
clergy declared that lifelong penance and continence
were to be the punishments applied to those who sinned
with two sisters. They also passed a canon setting forth
that in case a man committed fornication, and his brother
afterwards married the woman ignorant of his connection with her, severe penance was to be imposed on the
sinner who, in addition to his fornication, allowed his
brother to be deceived.[29]

It was decided at the Synod of Bourges in 1030 that
no one could marry the widow of a relative "because a
man and wife, legitimately joined, are of one body";
hence a relative by marriage was in reality a relative
by blood.[30] This is the earliest clear statement of the
theory underlying prohibition of marriage among affines to be found in the enactments of synods and councils.

The Synod of Vienne and Tours stipulated excommunication as the penalty to be imposed on any who
contracted marriage with a blood relative or with a
person with whom a blood relative had enjoyed carnal
relations.[31]

In an enactment of the Synod of London in 1125 is
found the first synodal legislation applying the seventh

---

[27] *Ibid.*, IV, 50.   [28] *Ibid.*, 371.   [29] *Ibid.*, 557.
[30] Mansi, *Sacrorum Conciliorum Collectio*, XIX, 505.
[31] Hefele, *Conciliengeschichte*, IV, 841–42.

degree as the limit to affines as well as to those related
by blood. It was ordained that "we forbid marriages to
be contracted between relatives or those joined in affinity up to the seventh generation; if, indeed, any have
so joined they are to be separated." [32] Another London
synod, held in the year 1200, promulgated a canon stip-
ulating that "no man may marry a blood relative of a
former wife and no woman may marry a relative of a
former husband." [33]

In the case of affinity as in that of consanguinity, the
Fourth Lateran Council marked an epoch in that it
abolished affinity of the "second and third kinds." The
distinction between the various "kinds" of affinity was
apparently not maintained by the official legislative or-
gans of the Church but was rather a result of the deduc-
tions of the canonists.

PAPAL DECRETALS

The first genuine papal decretal in respect to affinity
was that of Gregory the Great, who decided that a
woman joined to a man in copulation belonged thence-
forth to his kindred, and this relationship continued
even after the death of the husband.[34] He also held that
in the event of a second marriage the ties of kinship
created by the first marriage endured and precluded
marriage between relatives by the first marriage with
relatives by the second union.[35] Gregory II, in explain-

---

[32] *Ibid.*, V, 391.   [33] *Ibid.*, 797.

[34] Mansi, *Sacrorum Conciliorum Collectio*, X, 444; Gratianus, *Decretum*, Causa XXXV, Q. X, c. 1. The decretals cited by Gratian ante-
dating this enactment of Gregory are spurious. See P. Jaffé, *Regesta Pontificum Romanorum* (Leipzig, 1885), Nos. 37, 201, 206.

[35] Mansi, *Sacrorum Conciliorum Collectio*, X, 444; Gratianus, *Decretum*, Causa XXXV, Q. V, c. 3, 4.

ing the degrees of relationship, declared that "you call them relatives who pertain to the man from the side of his wife, or from the side of the wife to the husband; the most apparent reason is because the man and his wife are one body, and, according to Divine sentence, she contributes to him and he to her. Therefore, I and the sister of my wife will be in the first degree, her son and I are in the second, her grandson and I in the third, and so on it is to be counted in the descendants from both the man and the wife." [36]

Nicholas I quoted the Synod of New Caesarea to the effect that anyone who successively married two brothers or two sisters was to be submitted to the pains of excommunication until the illicit union was sundered.[37] In assigning proper penance to be performed by those entering upon incestuous marriages, Nicholas included those who married two sisters, mother-in-law, or stepmother among those who were to undergo the first category of penance as outlined in the section on consanguinity.[38]

A very inclusive prohibition of marriages among affines was issued by Alexander II. He replied in answer to an inquiry that a woman married to a man, even though he were a foreigner, became a member of his kindred, and this relationship persisted even after the death of the husband, nor was it dissolved by the contraction of a subsequent marriage.[39]

Clement III was called upon to decide what was indeed a complicated case. Two men who were unrelated married sisters. One of the sisters died without off-

---

[36] Migne, *P.L.*, LXXXIX, 524–25.   [37] *Ibid.*, CXIX, 918.
[38] See *supra*, 19–20.   [39] Migne, *P.L.*, CXLVI, 1411.

spring, whereupon her husband contracted another marriage. A son, born of this union, was later married to a daughter of the other sister. Children were born of this union, and after a considerable lapse of time the marriage was impugned. The local ecclesiastical authorities were unable to decide the matter and submitted the case to the pope for adjudication. The pope held that the marriage was indeed illegal, but those who now questioned the validity of the marriage could be considered suspect and debarred from testimony.[40] The same pontiff, in another decision, held that if anyone confessed to having known carnally a relative of his wife prior to their marriage, the marriage was not to be nullified on that account.[41]

An interesting decretal in regard to affinity was issued by Celestine III. In deciding a case wherein a man had carnal intercourse with his daughter-in-law after the death of his wife and then married another woman, even though his sin was publicly known, the pope took the position that this second marriage was not to be dissolved; but in the event that the man survived his second wife he was henceforth to eschew marriage.[42]

Innocent III (1198–1216) decided that where a man who was engaged to a girl below marriageable age had carnally known her mother and then, after the lapse of some time, had the same relations with his betrothed, all parties were to maintain perpetual continence. However, if it could be shown that the young girl had refrained from carnal intercourse with the man as soon as

[40] *Ibid.*, CCIV, 1484; S. Baluze (ed.), *Miscellanea* (Luca, 1761–1764), III, 379.

[41] Migne, *P.L.*, CCIV, 1487.

[42] *Decretales Gregorii IX Papae*, Lib. IV, Tit. XIII, c. 4.

she learned of his relations with her mother, she was to be permitted to contract a legitimate marriage with another man.[43]

In the legislation of synods and councils as well as in the decretals of the popes, nothing was stated as to the various "kinds" of affinity. The distinction between the various "kinds" of affinity found its most complete expression in the *Summa* of Bernard of Pavia. He declared that there were three "kinds" of affinity. The first "kind" was the "relationship between me and the relatives of my wife to which I attain through the medium of my wife; similarly, between my wife and my relatives there is affinity of the first kind." The second "kind" of affinity was begotten through the medium of two persons. It was the relationship "between me and the wife of the relative of my wife, who attains to me by the medium of my wife and her relationship; likewise, between my wife and the husbands of my relatives." The first and second "kinds" could exist together. Thus, if A's sister were to marry, her husband would be related to A in the first "kind" of affinity. Were she to die and her husband to marry another, the husband would continue to be related to A in the first "kind," whereas his second wife and her relatives would be related to A in the second "kind" of affinity. The third "kind" of affinity was produced through the mediation of three persons.[44]

These senseless distinctions were abolished by the Fourth Lateran Council. Canon L set forth that "it ought not to be judged blameworthy if human statutes be varied according to the change of the times, espe-

[43] *Ibid.*, c. 8.   [44] Bernardus Papiensis, *Summa*, 168–69.

cially when urgent necessity or evident usefulness demands this: Indeed, God himself changed some things
in the New Testament which he had ordained in the
Old. Therefore, prohibitions for contracting in marriage in the second and third kinds of affinity and prohibitions of offspring, begotten from second marriages,
to be married to the relatives of the first spouse, frequently induced difficulty and brought forth danger to
souls, so that . . . we decree, by this present constitution, that those so related are to be freely joined." [45]

The Impediment of Public Honesty

The impediment known as "public honesty" prevented marriage to one who previously had been betrothed to a relative. It was so called because such a
marriage was regarded as repellent to the moral sense
of the Christian community, but the law was not completely developed during the period under discussion.

The first legislation on this subject was a decretal of
Benedict I (574–578), which seems to be genuine, in
answer to a question propounded in regard to a girl betrothed to a youth who died before the marriage could
be performed. The girl upon the death of her betrothed
desired to marry his brother, and the question was submitted to the pope for decision. Benedict held that they
could be married because no relationship had been contracted between the girl and her first-betrothed since "a
man and a woman cannot be made one body unless they
cling to each other in carnal union. . . . Kinship is
called by words but it is not effected by words; nor does

[45] Hefele and Leclerq, *Histoire des conciles*, V, Pt. II, 1372.

a kiss engender kinship since it brings no mixture of blood." [46]

Gregory I wrote to the Emperor Maurice regarding a somewhat similar case, but his decision was opposed to that of Benedict. He decided that "who takes in marriage the girl betrothed to his relative, is anathematized together with all consenting to this because, according to the Law of God, it is decreed that the custom of Divine Law is to call those who are betrothed relatives." [47]

The next legislation in regard to this matter is found in a decretal of Benedict VI (972–974). A certain John betrothed his daughter to one Stephen, but the man died before the marriage was celebrated. John then wished to marry her to Stephen's brother and applied to his local ecclesiastical authorities for permission; they in turn submitted the case to the adjudication of the pope. The pontiff decided that the marriage would be legal since no relationship was engendered by the betrothal.[48]

There were two important decisions by Clement III. In one case a man confessed that, after having been betrothed to a girl below the marital age, he carnally knew her sister. The girl's parents wanted the marriage to the betrothed to be carried out as planned, and a local archdeacon compelled the errant man to marry her. The pope decided, in answer to a query from the bishop,

---

[46] Migne, *P.L.*, LXXII, 683; Gratianus, *Decretum*, Causa XXVII, Q. II, c. 18.

[47] Gratianus, *Decretum*, Causa XXVII, Q. II, c. 12. Accepted as genuine by Jaffé, *Regesta*, No. 1856a.

[48] Migne, *P.L.*, LXXII, 683; Gratianus, *Decretum*, Causa XXVII, Q. II, c. 18.

that "since the man was incriminated solely by his own confession, he was not to refrain from marriage." [49]

The same pontiff was called upon to decide another difficult case. A nobleman contracted a betrothal, in behalf of his son, with a girl of noble birth who was still too young to marry. He then took the young girl into his house as his ward, and after she had lived there about four years the nobleman's wife died. Soon after the death of his wife the widower, "with diabolical instigation," slept with his son's betrothed and even publicly treated her as his wife. The pope ordered that he be compelled to separate from her at once, but he did not issue a decision as to whether or not the son could marry the girl in accordance with the terms of the original betrothal. [50]

Innocent III decreed that in a case where a man was engaged to a woman and subsequently married her relative, the man was to do penance, and he and his wife were to maintain continence if possible; but in the event that continence was impossible, they were to be allowed to continue in marriage. [51]

When we turn to the canonists, we do not find unanimity of opinion, although the balance seems to lean to the doctrine that marriage with a party who had been previously betrothed to a relative should be avoided. Gratian cited an apocryphal bull of Julius (337–352) declaring that a man could not marry the betrothed of his relative. [52] He also cited Gregory to substantiate the same principle. [53] He included the answers of Nicholas I

---

[49] Migne, *P.L.*, CCIV, 1495.   [50] *Ibid.*, 1483.

[51] *Decretales Gregorii IX Papae*, Lib. IV, Tit. XIII, c. 6.

[52] Gratianus, *Decretum*, Causa XXVII, Q. II, c. 15.   [53] *Ibid.*, c. 14.

(858–867) to the Bulgarians to establish the point that consent was the essence of marriage.[54]

Roland distinguished between two phases in marriage. They were the beginning of marriage, accomplished by the mutual consent of the parties, and the consummation of the marriage, engendered by carnal copulation. Entrance upon the first phase was deemed sufficient to preclude subsequent marriage with a relative of one of the parties to the first "union." [55] Stephen took the same position.[56] Bernard of Pavia, however, declared that "betrothal is no affinity unless coition intervened." [57]

SPIRITUAL RELATIONSHIP

The earliest extant legislation in respect to spiritual relationship is a decretal of Deusdedit (615–618) issued between the years 615 and 618. In answer to an inquiry he declared that "no one ought to give to his son in marriage the daughter whom he received from the Sacred Font because, by Divine Sentence, they are found to be relatives." He went on to decree that "if anyone be joined in that sin, he will be abominated by the Catholic Church." In the event that the sinner sundered the union, seven years of penance were to be undertaken by both the guilty parties and their abettors.[58]

In a canon promulgated by the Trullan Synod in 692, it was ordered that anyone who raised children from the Sacred Font could not marry the mother of

---

[54] *Ibid.*, c. 2.   [55] Magister Rolandus, *Summa,* 129–30.
[56] Stephanus Tornacensis, *Summa,* 232.
[57] Bernardus Papiensis, *Summa,* 168.
[58] Gratianus, *Decretum,* Causa XXX, Q. III, c. 3.

these children since "the spiritual relationship was of
more importance than the worldly one." [59] The Roman
Synod, held *ca.* 725, threatened anathema against one
who married his spiritual mother.[60]

Pope Zacharias issued two decretals relating to spiritual kinship. He decreed seven years of penance for anyone who married his spiritual daughter; and the marriage of a man to a girl whom his father raised from the
Sacred Font was to be dissolved, and children begotten
of the illicit union were to be barred from marriage.[61]

The Synod of Compiègne, held in the year 757 or
758, ordained that "if anyone has led his stepson or
stepdaughter to confirmation, he dare no longer have
intercourse with his wife and can marry no one else." [62]

Nicholas I in his famous "Answers to the Bulgarians"
declared that "a man ought to esteem him who received
him from the Sacred Font as a father, just as the spirit
is more important than the flesh, because the paternity
is spiritual and an adoption according to God; hence,
the spiritual father is to be greatly esteemed in all
things by the spiritual son." The pontiff pointed out,
by way of example, that Mark had been the spiritual
son of Peter and had obeyed his spiritual parent in all
things. While there was no blood relationship between
spiritual relatives "because the spirit knows nothing of
the things which are of blood," there was "kindness,
holy communion, and more especially spiritual proximity." Hence, declared the pope, "Marriage is not to be
thought of between them, since the Roman laws per-

---

[59] Hefele, *Conciliengeschichte*, III, 337.   [60] *Ibid.*, 362.
[61] Migne, *P.L.*, LXXXIX, 958–60.
[62] Hefele, *Conciliengeschichte*, III, 595.

mit marriage neither between those who are sons by
nature nor those who are sons by law." [63]

The same pontiff decided that a man could not be
married to a woman who was his co-mother.[64] A woman
was a co-mother of him whose daughter she raised from
the Sacred Font.[65] The Synod of Worms adopted a
canon which threatened anathema against anyone who
married his co-mother or spiritual child.[66]

Stephen VIII *ca.* 939 decreed that anathema was to
be pronounced on all who married their spiritual moth-
ers or daughters.[67] Urban II held that whoever successively married two co-mothers committed a crime which
was to be punished by a most heavy penance, and he
also held that a husband and wife were not to act jointly
as sponsors to a child at baptism or confirmation since
this brought them into the category of spiritual relatives. Although this impediment was not to void their
marriage, they were to refrain sedulously from joint
participation in these ceremonies, "so that the purity of
spiritual paternity may be preserved immune from all
ruin and infamy." [68]

Clement III issued a decretal ordering the dissolution of a marriage between co-parents.[69] Celestine III
also decreed that marriages of spiritual relatives were to
be dissolved.[70]

[63] Migne, *P.L.*, CXIX, 979.   [64] *Ibid.*, 1128.
[65] C. D. Du Cange, *Glossarium mediae et infimae Latinitatis* (Niort,
1883), *sub commater* (II, 469).
[66] Hefele, *Conciliengeschichte*, IV, 371.
[67] Mansi, *Sacrorum Conciliorum Collectio*, XVIII, 378.
[68] Migne, *P.L.*, CLI, 529. Alexander III held that if this were done
inadvertently the marriage should not be dissolved. *Decretales Gregorii
IX Papae*, Lib. IV, Tit. XI, c. 2.
[69] Migne, *P.L.*, CCIV, 1487.   [70] *Ibid.*, CCVI, 1255.

The ceremonies of baptism and confirmation were construed as rebirths, that is, by baptism one was born into the Christian community, and by confirmation one was born into the Church.[71] Hence, the sponsors of a child at either of these ceremonies became its parents, indeed, parents of a higher type than physical parents.[72]

Although the relationships contracted by participation in the ceremonies of baptism and confirmation operated to preclude marriage between the parties immediately involved, there is no evidence to substantiate a supposition that the relationship thus contracted was extended to the seventh degree, as was the case with the relationships of consanguinity and affinity. There are some instances of enforcement of these provisions, but their rigor was considerably mitigated by relaxation in the form of papal dispensations.

Procedure in Matrimonial Cases

The procedure followed in matrimonial cases was practically the same as the canonical procedure in criminal cases, but certain specific enactments somewhat modified it.[73]

Alexander II in 1063, in deciding a particular case which had been submitted to him, ordained that "on no account may you presume to dismiss the wife whom you now have, or take another until a council of religious bishops examines the case."[74] The Synod of Rouen in 704 ordered that if anyone alleged irregularity in his marital relationship as a pretext to separate from his

[71] Stephanus Tornacensis, *Summa*, 241.   [72] *Ibid.*
[73] Bernardus Papiensis, *Summa*, 184.
[74] Migne, *P.L.*, CXLVI, 1387.

wife, he was to be compelled to substantiate his contentions.[75]

Eugenius *ca.* 1150 decreed that "when anyone is to
be separated because of the relationship by kindred, or
consanguinity, the facts ought to be affirmed by three
witnesses who survive from this kindred, or by two or
three older and more trustworthy witnesses of this
place. The proof of witnesses ought to be made by two-
fold oath. The witnesses ought to swear that they are
led to taking this oath neither by hate nor friendship,
nor by gold or any other business in which they are involved. Afterwards they ought to swear that they have
learned the truth of the matter from their elders and
that it is as they swear." [76] Alexander III declared that
if it were proved that witnesses in a matrimonial case
had been corrupted by money, their testimony was to
be repudiated.[77]

Clement III issued a number of important decretals
relative to the procedure in matrimonial cases. He ordained that a written document, presumably a genealogy, was not to be taken as conclusive testimony in
determining consanguinity. He also held that if anyone
had an opportunity to testify in a marital case and maintained silence, he was to be debarred from subsequently
impugning the marriage in question unless he learned
of new facts since the first trial of the case.[78]

The same pontiff, in deciding another case, held that
witnesses were to be admitted to determine the degree
of relationship, and that both sides were to be per-

---

[75] Hefele, *Conciliengeschichte*, V, 35.
[76] Migne, *P.L.*, CLXXX, 1565.
[77] *Decretales Gregorii IX Papae*, Lib. II, Tit. XX, c. 9.
[78] Migne, *P.L.*, CCIV, 1490.

mitted to produce witnesses. He also held that if an exception on the grounds of consanguinity was interposed in a marital case, the exception, if substantiated, was to have the effect of automatically quashing the proceedings.[79] Thus, let us say, if a man were accused of adultery by his wife, and in the process of the trial alleged that blood relationship existed between him and his wife, this allegation, if substantiated, would void the proceedings in adultery and would also, of course, render the separation of the parties mandatory.

The laws imposing the impediments to marriage were developed in all their essential details by the end of the period under discussion. Precedents for the legislation of the Church were found in the Roman law as well as in some passages of the Scriptures. A large number of synodal enactments and papal decretals were issued defining the law and giving instructions for its enforcement. By erroneously combining the Roman law relating to incest with the laws governing intestate succession, the Christian legislation forbade marriages of relatives up to the seventh degree. This provision was supplanted by the enactment of the Fourth Lateran Council which stipulated the fourth degree as the limit within which relationship was to be reckoned. After considerable controversy the canonists evolved a system by which the degree of relationship was to be determined.

[79] *Decretales Gregorii IX Papae,* Lib. II, Tit. X, c. 1.

CHAPTER IV

ENFORCEMENT OF THE LAW BY POPE NICHOLAS I

THE first recorded instance of papal intervention in a marital case involving the impediment of relationship was that of Pope Vigilius (537–555). Theodebert, King of Austrasia, violated the law by contracting marriage with the widow of his brother. In response to an inquiry of Caesarius, Bishop of Arles, as to the penance to be imposed on the transgressor, the pontiff declared that his guilt was to be expiated "by a no little affliction of the body." The prelate was ordered to instruct the king in the ways of the law so that he would not be beguiled into such errors.[1]

During the pontificate of Nicholas I papal intervention was necessitated in several cases. It was said that the pope sent his legates to Sardinia "where the judges of the Island, together with the people submitted to their government, contracted incestuous marriages with their nearest of kin and affinity, as they were accustomed to do in the times of the Lord Pope Gregory IV." The pope absolutely forbade the practice on pain of ecclesiastical censures.[2]

The most celebrated marital case in which Nicholas insisted upon the observance of the canons involved

[1] Migne, *P.L.*, LXIX, 21.
[2] *Vita Nicholai Papae*, in *Liber Pontificalis* (ed. Duchesne), II, 102.

Lothair II, King of Lotharingia. The matter of incest was an important feature of this case since it was the ostensible reason which induced the king to repudiate his legitimate wife and espouse another.

Lothair married Teutberga, daughter of Boso of Burgundy, in 857. The following year, however, the king "began to seek opportunities to separate Queen Teutberga from his association . . . because of Waldrada who had been his concubine when he was a youth in his father's house." Charges of a most disgraceful nature were brought against the unhappy queen. It was charged that she had indulged in an unnatural and incestuous intercourse with her brother, as a result of which she had become pregnant and had been delivered by an abortion prior to her marriage to Lothair. The difficulty with this accusation was the fact that Lothair at the time of his marriage to Teutberga either expressly or tacitly admitted her virginity. A theory of virgin birth with occult aid then was advanced to obviate the inconsistency of the charge, and Hincmar, the doughty archbishop of Rheims, felt called upon to refute this contention with a formidable array of anatomical knowledge.[3]

Confronted with these grave charges, the queen appeared before an assembly of nobles and ecclesiastics and offered to purge herself by submitting a champion to the ordeal of hot water. The champion successfully underwent the test, and the queen was pronounced absolved from the accusations.[4]

---

[3] Regino Prumiensis, *Chronicon*, in *M.G.H.*, *SS.*, I, 571.

[4] *Ibid.*; Hincmarus, *De Divortio Lotharii et Tetbergae*, in Migne, *P.L.*, CCXV, 629.

Her triumph was short lived. Lothair, impelled by
the wiles of Waldrada, whom "he esteemed with a
great love," [5] and abetted by his favorite counselors,
Liutfrid and Vultarius,[6] persisted in his desire for an
annulment. Guntharius, the archbishop of Cologne, was
won over to his cause, probably in the hope that his
niece would become the bride of the king in the event
that a separation were decreed. Guntharius succeeded
in inveigling his guileless colleague, Thietgaudus, the
archbishop of Trèves, to acquiesce in the plan.[7]

Under the leadership of the two archbishops a council was convoked at Aix-la-Chapelle in 862, to which
the queen was canonically summoned.[8] Witnesses were
produced for the prosecution, who submitted documents of a dubious character ostensibly substantiating
the charges of incest as well as of other enormities. The
obsequious prelates, after reading a number of canons
pertaining to the crime of incest, not only permitted the
king to separate from his wife, but actually forbade him
to have further marital relations with her. In addition
to the sentence of separation the council decided that
the queen should do penance.[9]

Not long after the conclusion of the council it was
reported that the queen had secretly confessed to the
crimes of which she had been accused.[10] Another council
then was convoked at Aix, "where the king voiced his
complaint, wherein was contained how, in the case of

[5] Regino Prumiensis, *Chronicon*, in *M.G.H., SS.*, I, 571.

[6] Hincmarus, *Annales*, in *M.G.H., SS.*, I, 458.

[7] Regino Prumiensis, *Chronicon*, in *M.G.H., SS.*, I, 571.

[8] Hincmarus, *Annales*, in *M.G.H., SS.*, I, 458.

[9] Regino Prumiensis, *Chronicon*, in *M.G.H., SS.*, I, 571–72.

[10] Hincmarus, *De Divortio*, in Migne, *P.L.*, CCXV, 630.

the woman, Teutberga by name, he was defrauded by
the arguments of abandoned men." [11] He "began with
a sad voice," reported prelates who were present, "so
that we could not follow without weeping and sadness." In addition to the contention that he had married Teutberga at the insistence of others for the sake of
political advantage, Lothair went on to declare that
Teutberga "with unmitigated and continual prayers desired to be released from the conjugal chain, that is to
say, the marital couch, in order to receive the veil and
deserve to serve Christ." [12] The council then declared
that the erstwhile queen was not "a suitable and legitimate wife," and Lothair, who tearfully avowed that he
was unable to maintain continence, was granted permission to marry Waldrada.[13]

The repudiated queen took refuge with King Charles
the Bald, who treated her well and assigned the revenues from the monastery of Avenai for her support.[14]
The attention of Pope Nicholas was drawn to the affair by letters from Lothair, wherein was contained the
request that the pope send legates to review the case.[15]
The brother of Teutberga also wrote to the pope, informing him of the treatment which had been meted
out to his sister.[16]

On November 23, 862, the pope wrote to Lothair
declaring that, while he had been prevented by the
press of business from promptly complying with the

[11] Regino Prumiensis, *Chronicon*, in *M.G.H., SS.*, I, 572.
[12] Hincmarus, *De Divortio*, in Migne, *P.L.*, CCXV, 631.
[13] Regino Prumiensis, *Chronicon*, in *M.G.H., SS.*, I, 572.
[14] Hincmarus, *Annales*, in *M.G.H., SS.*, I, 467.
[15] Migne, *P.L.*, CXIX, 798, 800.
[16] Regino Prumiensis, *Chronicon*, in *M.G.H., SS.*, I, 572.

royal request for the dispatch of legates, he was now
ready to attend to the matter. He informed the king
that he was sending Bishops Rhadoald and John to convoke and preside over a synod. In addition to the
clergy from Lothair's realm, the projected assembly
was to include two bishops from the kingdom of Charles
the Bald and two from the jurisdiction of Louis the
German.[17]

On the same day the pontiff wrote to Charles the
Bald. The epistle opened with a strong assertion of the
papal prerogative. "This holy and principal seat, to
which is committed the anxiety and care of the Lord's
fold in all parts of the world," wrote the pope, "man-
ages to order and to carry out what it wishes to accom-
plish by authority alone." To the See of Peter was
committed the duty to "deliberate for making amends
with the censure of justice in those things which were
done falsely and abusively." Charles then was informed
of the projected synod and directed to send two bishops
from his domains. The pope declared that he expected
both Teutberga and Waldrada to appear before the assembly, composed of the most discreet and learned
clergy, who were to "examine and pronounce judgment
according to God and the venerable institutions of the
Holy Fathers," so that "in all things which there were
to be decided, righteousness should thrive, justice prevail, and truth shine out." [18] The Emperor Louis II
then was informed of the pope's plan to send legates to
Lothair's kingdom and was directed graciously to receive the papal representatives.[19]

[17] Migne, *P.L.*, CXIX, 798.   [18] *Ibid.*, 799.
[19] *Ibid.*, 799–800.

In a letter also dated November 23, 862, the pope addressed all archbishops and bishops who were to participate in the forthcoming synod. The prelates were commended for their good conduct in that hitherto they "had cherished the things that ought to be cherished" and had not been "moved by terrors of any kind or inclined from the path of justice even by lavish rewards and increases in honors." They were admonished to be equally scrupulous and fearless in the matter which soon was to be submitted to their decision. After briefly reviewing the king's marital case and explaining the necessity of remanding it to them for adjudication, the pontiff ordered them to judge with his legates "without the strain of mortification, the ferment of treachery, or the nourishment of hate which could deter men from the way of truth and, for shame, even from the path of righteousness." [20]

By the spring of 863 the legates were ready to undertake their mission, and in a letter of April the pope transmitted their instructions to them. They were directed to convene the synod at Metz, but in the event that the prelates failed to assemble or Lothair contumaciously refused to appear, they were ordered to go wherever he might be. If the king obdurately refrained from submission to their jurisdiction, he was to be excommunicated. On the other hand, if they were successful in organizing a synod with the king in attendance, they were instructed first to examine Lothair's marriage to Waldrada to determine if, aside from the king's separation from his first wife, the nuptials had been canonically performed. If there were no canonical impedi-

[20] *Ibid.*, 801–802.

ment to their marriage, the legates were to turn their attention to the position of Teutberga and determine on what grounds her marriage had been invalidated by the local clergy. The pontiff declared that it had been rumored that Lothair desired separation from her because of fear, and if this allegation were correct, the pope deemed the king worthy of censure in that he had "subordinated the love of God to the love of the world" and had been "thrown into the pit by the fear of man." The legates were ordered carefully to examine this contention.[21] If Lothair and Waldrada were declared living in concubinage, either because of the illegality of the annulment of the king's first marriage or because some other impediment precluded legitimate union, they were to be required to separate immediately and do condign penance for their sin.[22]

The instructions further set forth that Teutberga had complained several times that she had "confessed crimes because of duress and force." This allegation was to be fully investigated. The legates were to ascertain if violence had been applied against the former queen and if the testimony of false witnesses or the charges of her enemies had been utilized to obtain her condemnation. After conducting the examination in accordance with the papal instructions, the legates were "to render justice according to the standard of equity lest she be oppressed by the weight of injustice."[23]

Shortly after receiving their instructions, the legates began their journey. After passing through the lands of the emperor, they arrived at Soissons, where they were hospitably received by Charles the Bald. After effect-

[21] Ibid., 1179–80.   [22] Ibid.   [23] Ibid.

ing the reconciliation of Charles with Baldwin, who had married his daughter without parental permission, the papal emissaries proceeded to Metz, where the synod was convoked according to directions; no clergy from the kingdom of Louis the German, however, attended.[24]

Unfortunately for Nicholas' hopes for an equitable decision, the apostolic representatives, "corrupted by gifts and concealing the letters of the Lord Apostle, carried out nothing concerning those things which were committed to them, according to the sacred authority," [25] but "debauched by money, they favored iniquity more than equity." [26] They acquiesced in the *status quo* of the affair and contented themselves with exacting a promise from the king that he would take no further steps in the matter without the permission of another synod.[27]

The legates further advised the king to send Guntharius and Thietgaudus to Rome to justify to Nicholas their invalidation of the marriage.[28] The papal emissaries thereupon returned to Rome and rendered an account of their stewardship, with the result that they were anathematized by the indignant pope.[29]

In October, 863, the archbishops arrived at Rome and at once were granted a preliminary audience, wherein they attempted to vindicate their reputations by reading various documents pertaining to the case.[30] On

---

[24] Hincmarus, *Annales*, in *M.G.H., SS.*, I, 460.   [25] *Ibid.*

[26] Regino Prumiensis, *Chronicon*, in *M.G.H., SS.*, I, 572.

[27] *Ibid.*, 572–73.

[28] *Ibid.; Vita Nicholai Papae*, in *Liber Pontificalis*, II, 160.

[29] Hincmarus, *Annales*, in *M.G.H., SS.*, I, 460.

[30] *Vita Nicholai Papae*, in *Liber Pontificalis*, II, 160.

October 30 a dramatic answer was given to their contentions. To the Roman clergy gathered in council at the Lateran Palace, the pope announced that the Synod of Metz, "which violated the orders of the Apostolic See . . . we order quashed for eternity and considered just as the Robber Synod of Ephesus . . . and we decree that it be eternally damned by apostolic authority; nor indeed, is it to be called a synod, but we direct that it be called an abettor of adultery and a prostitute." [31]

The pontiff then turned his attention to the offending metropolitans. After stating that the prelates had rendered a full account to him concerning their proceedings, the pope ordained that "in all respects we find the apostolic and canonical decrees exceeded and the balance of equity flouted; hence, we sentence them to remain deposed from all sacerdotal offices and declare them deprived of all episcopal functions." [32]

The pope sent letters to the prelates of France, Germany, and Italy, informing them of the deprivation of the offending archbishops.[33] A special letter of the same tenor also was sent to Archbishop Hincmar.[34] To the prelates of Germany the pope wrote that "the indignity which was committed with Teutberga and Waldrada by King Lothair, if, indeed, he can be called king who did not resist the temptations of the body with any saving rigor, but conceded to his illicit impulses with slippery sloth," was now a matter of common knowledge. Rumors had come to the Apostolic See that the errant king was abetted in his derelictions by the vicious coun-

---

[31] Hincmarus, *Annales*, in *M.G.H., SS.*, I, 460–61.   [32] *Ibid.*, 461.
[33] Mansi, *Sacrorum Conciliorum Collectio*, XV, 649–50.
[34] Migne, *P.L.*, CXV, 1213–14.

cils of some of his prelates, but the pope declared that
he had been reluctant to believe these reports. However, with the appearance of the archbishops at Rome
all his doubts had been removed. The deprivation of
the prelates then was announced, and the clergy were
ordered to withdraw their recognition of them.[35]

Letters subsequently were sent to King Lothair in
which he was bitterly censured for causing the ruin of
others by his lust. "Since you consented to accede to the
impulses of your body, and, having relaxed the reins
of pleasure, threw yourself in the lake of misery and in
the mire of filth for the sake of pleasure," wrote the
pope, "you, having been set up for the government of
the people, instead, effected the ruin of many." The
deprivation of the archbishops was proclaimed, and
their fate was cited as a proof of the papal contention
that Lothair's sin was beguiling many to deviate from
the path of rectitude.[36] In an ensuing letter the pope
forbade the king to nominate any new incumbents for
the vacated archbishoprics.[37]

The pontiff's next step was an attempt to win over
the errant king by persuasion. In a letter of March 30,
864, Adonis, Archbishop of Vienne, was directed "to
exhort King Lothair by pastoral watchfulness, sacred
warnings, and divine incantations because of the dismissal of his first wife and espousal of a second."
"There was not," declared the pope, "in this inconti-
nence of juvenile pleasure that for which he should lose
the Kingdom of Glory forever." Lothair was not consciously choosing the way to perdition, and with guidance and proper advice the pope expressed belief that

[35] *Ibid.*, CXIX, 868–69.   [36] *Ibid.*, 869.   [37] *Ibid.*

the errant king would soon give heed to the exhortations of the Holy See.[38]

The next correspondence in the case was a letter of May 12, 864, directed to Louis the German, who recently had sent an emissary to the Holy See denying his complicity in his nephew's marital affairs. The pope answered that he was angry with Louis not "because he consented to the illicit marriage but because, although not consenting, he did not forbid it; and it is not sufficient for salvation to refrain from evil if we do not do good." His relationship to the transgressor was declared to have accentuated the guilt of indifference. "Since Christ is truth," continued the pope, "whosoever does not openly fight for truth denies Christ before men." [39]

In the meantime the deposed archbishops had not been idle. They returned to their sees, and Guntharius even presumed to celebrate mass despite his sentence of deprivation.[40] The two appealed to the Emperor Louis, claiming that they had been illegally deprived and calling attention to the dangers that threatened temporal rulers if the pope could, with impunity, degrade prelates.[41]

Their protests appear in a letter which they probably sent to Nicholas and which is preserved in the "Annals of Fulda." [42] They claimed that the pope publicly had expressed approval of their actions on the occasion of their first audience with him prior to the assembly of the Lateran Synod.[43] They complained that, after a

[38] *Ibid.*, 869–70.
[40] *Annales Fuldenses*, in *M.G.H., SS.*, I, 378.
[42] Hincmarus, *Annales*, in *M.G.H., SS.*, I, 463.
[39] *Ibid.*, 872–73.
[41] *Ibid.*, 377–78.
[43] *Ibid.*

long and unseemly delay, "we were led into your presence, suspecting nothing adverse; there, after the doors
were locked, and after a conspiracy was consummated
in the manner of thieves, and after a mixed crowd of
laymen and clergy were collected, you tried violently
to oppress us, separated as we were from our clergy and
laity by a great distance. Without a synod or a canonical
examination, without accuser or witnesses against us,
without disputation, and without our own confession,
you desired to damn us by your arbitrariness and tyr-
anny alone, entirely without the consent of all present
and in the absence of our colleagues and of other metropolitans and bishops." [44]

Louis was induced to espouse the cause of the Lo-
tharingian prelates. He entered Rome with an army and
proceeded to the Basilica of the Blessed Peter at the
time "the clergy and Roman people, with crosses and
litanies, were coming there to celebrate the Feast in
Memory of the Blessed Peter. And when they began
to ascend the steps before the Basilica . . . they were
struck to the ground and beaten by divers blows, and the
crosses and standards were broken. Those who could
escape fled; in the tumult the miraculous and venerated
cross, made by Helena of holy memory, in which was
placed the wood of the true cross . . . was broken and
thrown into the mud from which it was collected and
restored to custody by men of England." Nicholas
was forced to take refuge in St. Peter's, where he tarried
two days and nights without food and drink.[45]

It was alleged in the meantime that the man who had

---

[44] *Annales Fuldenses*, in *M.G.H., SS.*, I, 377–78.
[45] Hincmarus, *Annales*, in *M.G.H., SS.*, I, 463.

broken the cross suddenly died, and it was also reported
that the emperor was smitten with sickness. These alleged visitations were regarded, of course, as portents
of divine wrath at the sacrilege committed by the imperial soldiery; Louis made haste to send his wife to
Nicholas to intercede and induce him to return to the
Lateran. Her mission was successful, and the pope, after
his reinstatement, ordered the deposed archbishops who
had accompanied the emperor to return to Lothair's
kingdom. The emperor then withdrew to Ravenna,
where he celebrated Easter.[46] Guntharius and Thietgaudus subsequently returned to Rome and vainly
sought absolution.[47]

In the fall of 864 the pope resumed his efforts to induce Lothair to leave Waldrada and return to his legitimate wife. In an epistle dated September 17, 864, written to Franconus, Bishop of Tongernhe, he censured
him for not openly opposing the king's marital actions,
although commending him for refusing to have any
contact with the deposed archbishops. The bishop was
ordered to "seek the glory of King Lothair" and to
"care for his wound by admonishing, cajoling, and persuading, showing him both the shortness of the present
time and the pains of hell, and placing the heavenly
kingdom before his eyes." [48]

The archbishops and bishops of Lothair's kingdom
subsequently were addressed in a general letter. The
pope recalled his own labors in the case and complained
that "for shame, you did not indicate to us, sweating in
unremitted labors, whether or not you also labored
against the poison, although in writing you avowed that

[46] Ibid.   [47] Migne, P.L., CXIX, 1161–63.   [48] Ibid., 885–87.

you felt and held with us." He directed them to "banish sloth, cast aside servile fear, resume episcopal freedom, grasp the offices of curators and pastors, and approach the said king more frequently by preaching, humoring, and persuading, showing him the transitory character of this world's prosperity and preaching the joys of eternal mansions." Towards the close of the letter excommunication of the king was threatened in the event he did not prove amenable to their admonitions. "Shout," directed the pontiff in closing, "raise your voices like a trumpet and proclaim to him his sin," so that "if the king refuses to hearken to your pleadings, he himself will die; his blood will be on his head while you will have freed your souls." [49]

In 865 the case seemed likely to be settled in accordance with the wishes of the pope. Charles the Bald and Louis the German met at Tullei in February and discussed the difficulties in which Lothair was embroiled. They sent letters to him ordering him "to journey to Rome and at once make amends for what he had done to the Church contrary to human and divine laws." Lothair, "fearing that they wished to take his kingdom from him and divide it among themselves," [50] sent Liutfrid, his brother, to the Emperor Louis, asking for his intercession with the pope and his protection against the territorial ambitions of his two uncles.[51] Louis promised assistance and at once made known the wayward king's desire for absolution.[52]

Nicholas, in no mood for compromise, hastened to dispatch Arsenius, Bishop of Ortensi, to receive the re-

[49] *Ibid.*, 915–16.   [50] Hincmarus, *Annales*, in *M.G.H., SS.*, I, 467.
[51] *Ibid.*, 475.   [52] *Ibid.*, 476.

pentant ruler's submission. At the same time the legate
bore letters to Louis the German and Charles the Bald
as well as to their clergy, expressing "not apostolic
mercy and the usual terms of respect with which the
Roman bishops were accustomed to honor kings in their
letters but laden with evil menaces." After a preliminary interview with Louis the German, the legate met
Lothair at Gundulfi and offered him the choice of at
once dismissing Waldrada and returning to his legitimate wife or of suffering immediate excommunication.[53]

The king chose the first alternative; and the legate,
after receiving his promise to comply with the papal
mandates, proceeded in June of 865 into the kingdom
of Charles the Bald, from whose protection he received
the exiled queen, whom he escorted to Lothair. A council of clergy and nobles was hastily summoned, before
which twelve men, representing Lothair, swore on the
Gospels and relics that the king would treat Teutberga
as his wife and queen and would eschew the society of
Waldrada. Arsenius then committed Teutberga to the
protection of Lothair and announced that in the event
he subsequently proved recalcitrant he would be *ipso
facto* excommunicated. Waldrada was remanded to the
custody of the legate, who undertook to escort her to
Rome where she was to answer to the pope for her
sins.[54]

Hopes that the vexatious case had been settled were
soon rudely disrupted when it was learned that Waldrada had escaped from the surveillance of Arsenius and

[53] *Ibid.; Annales Fuldenses*, in *M.G.H., SS.*, I, 379.
[54] Hincmarus, *Annales*, in *M.G.H., SS.*, I, 468.

returned to her paramour. Nicholas immediately responded by excommunicating her in a letter dated February 2, 866. He pointed out that he visited this punishment upon her, not so much because of her adultery, as because she obdurately had remained impenitent and proposed to "remain in the filth of adultery, oblivious to sacred warnings and frequent exhortations." Despite the pope's labors in her behalf, she had refused to confess her sin and seek absolution from the See of Peter, which would be ready to "temper justice with mercy." [55]

"Not a little scandal is begotten in the Church of Christ," complained the pontiff; "the glory of the world is sought after; it dominates public affairs, and what is more grave, it is even known to prevail in pious places and among religious persons." Mild strictures also were cast on Teutberga's conduct. It was reported that she had entered upon the religious life, but she endeavored to "seek places where her access to King Lothair and that of the king to her could be easy." The letter closed with Waldrada's sentence. She was to be denied the sacraments of the Church and access to Christian edifices and was to be shunned by all Christians.[56] On June 13, 866, an identical letter was sent to the archbishops and bishops of Italy, Germany, Neustria, and the Gauls, so that all churchmen might be acquainted with the excommunication.[57]

Lothair was to be considered excommunicated if he failed to carry out his oath to Arsenius. The pope ap-

---

[55] Mansi, *Sacrorum Conciliorum Collectio*, XV, 381.
[56] *Ibid.*   [57] Migne, *P.L.*, CXIX, 971–73.

70 MEDIEVAL MARRIAGE LAWS

parently confirmed this sentence in a letter no longer extant, but no effort seems to have been made to put it into effect.[58]

The king apparently adopted the policy of coercing Teutberga into petitioning the pope, ostensibly on her own volition, to dissolve the marriage, for she wrote to him declaring that she wished to abdicate and enter a convent.[59] She also professed to regard her continued sterility as an evidence of God's displeasure at her union with Lothair and begged leave to come to Rome to submit her plea to the pope. Nicholas was not to be deceived. In his answer dated January 24, 867, he declared he had anticipated a statement of this kind in view of the "afflictions, intolerable oppressions, and violence by which she had been vexed." In consequence of the manifest coercion that had been applied, he refused to credit the queen's statements. In reply to her allegation that Waldrada was really Lothair's wife, he assured her that the king never would be permitted to marry this woman, even though Teutberga herself were dead. If she really wished to embrace the celibate life, the pope declared that he had no objection, but he could give his consent only on condition that Lothair also engaged to remain continent. The childlessness of the queen was ascribed by the pope to the sinfulness of her husband rather than to her own derelictions or to providential intervention. She further was directed not to come to Rome but was urged to constancy and courage in the face of her travails, since "better, indeed, it is that another kill you speaking the truth, than that you

---

[58] Hefele, *Conciliengeschichte*, IV, 303.
[59] Migne, *P.L.*, CXIX, 1136–38.

kill yourself speaking lies." "Be content," she was exhorted; "do not fear death for the sake of truth; since
Christ is truth, whoever dies for truth doubtless dies
for Christ." [60]

The following day the archbishops and bishops of
Lothair's realm were addressed by papal letters wherein
they were chided for their lethargy in the enforcement
of Waldrada's excommunication. They were ordered to
disseminate knowledge of her punishment as far as possible and to keep the Holy See informed as to the king's
conduct.[61]

On the same day letters were sent to Lothair, Charles,
and Louis. Lothair was told that at the news of his correction the pope had rejoiced and rendered thanks to
God; but adverse tidings subsequently made it necessary to "change our voices, and when we were disposed
to open our mouth in thanksgivings, we were compelled
to direct the power of speaking to lamentations and
chidings." The pontiff stated that he had received Teutberga's proposal of abdication, but reports carried by
pilgrims to Rome had convinced him that the queen's
depositions had been extorted. He berated the king for
inducing men to perjure themselves in his behalf, but
even this was of minor consequence compared with the
sin of involving thousands in wrongdoing by his example. The pope reiterated his dictum that permission
to marry Waldrada would never be granted, nor would
he agree to any project of separation from Teutberga
unless both she and the king freely manifested their desire to remain continent. The king was warned that
further disregard of the papal admonitions would re-

[60] *Ibid.*   [61] *Ibid.*, 1139–42.

sult in rigorous application of ecclesiastical censures.[62]

In his letter to King Charles, the pontiff truculently demanded that he desist from his reported arrangement with Lothair, under the terms of which Teutberga would be relegated to a nunnery while Lothair would remain with Waldrada.[63] Louis the German was cautioned in a milder vein against entering into a similar agreement.[64]

The case had reached the stage where any further attempt to persuade Lothair to change his course obviously was futile. Sterner measures were needed, and there can be little doubt but that Nicholas was ready to coerce the recalcitrant king by ecclesiastical censures, with the partition schemes of Charles and Louis affording adequate secular support in the background. However, Nicholas' death in 867 transferred the burden of enforcing the papal mandates to other shoulders.

Hadrian II (867–872), the successor of Nicholas, very soon after his elevation gave evidence of his intention to carry out his predecessor's policy in regard to the notorious marital case. Teutberga, apparently coerced by Lothair, came to Rome and appealed to the pope for a separation from her husband. She alleged that she was afflicted with bodily infirmities which incapacitated her for marital life. In addition, she professed "that she desired to cast aside the dignity and honor [of being queen] for the love of God and wished to submit the neck of her heart beneath the gentle yoke of Christ." [65]

Her avowals were respectfully heard by the pope and

[62] *Ibid.,* 1146.
[64] *Ibid.,* 1150–51.

[63] *Ibid.,* 1142–46.
[65] *Ibid.,* CXXII, 1259.

his advisers, but they made little impression. On December 14, 867, Hadrian addressed a letter to Lothair, wherein he recounted the pitiful abnegation of the queen. He pleaded with the recalcitrant king to "open the ear of his heart to the healing, key-bearing Peter speaking in us" and "hearken to those preaching . . . the things that were compatible with justice and more especially with righteousness."

Two grave sins had been committed by the king declared Hadrian. The first was his separation from his legitimate wife, while the second was his adherence to "that most rascally adultress, Waldrada." As to the queen's confessions at Rome, the pope declared he had diligently discussed them with his advisers, who proved to be in unanimity with him in refusing to consent to requests that were manifestly irreconcilable with the teachings of scripture.

Lothair was strongly urged to receive Teutberga again in his favor, to be treated as it beseemed a king to act toward his queen. If she delayed her return to him because of illness, he was directed to place at her disposal certain revenues of monasteries which he long had promised her in order that she might be supported in proper state.[66]

Early in 868 Hadrian had to warn both Louis the German and Charles the Bald to desist from their contemplated invasion of Lothair's realm.[67] The reason for the pope's action was his fear that such aggression would incite the Emperor Louis with a desire to share in the spoil. The result would be that his efforts against the

---

[66] *Ibid.*   [67] *Ibid.*, 1263.

Saracens who were making serious advances in Italy would be diverted to internecine strife.[68]

The next stage in the progress of the case was the change of heart on the part of Waldrada. Reports were transmitted to Rome by the emperor and others to the effect that she had repented and desired absolution. The reasons that prompted her sudden alteration of conduct are unknown, but it is possible that it was dictated solely by contrition. Hadrian made haste to grant the desired absolution. On February 12, 868, he wrote to the woman who so sorely had tried papal patience, declaring that "although you were held fast by the sin by which you were ensnared . . . we learn by the reports of many, and especially from the report of our most faithful son, Louis the Emperor . . . that you are said to have come to your senses and that you are reported to have abandoned the obstinacy in which you were entangled." "Rejoice," went on the pope, "freed from the chains of anathema and excommunication and returned to the fellowship of the united Christians." The pontiff felt bound, however, to warn her that if she returned to her paramour she again would be subjected to the penalties of the Church.[69] On the same day the archbishops in the kingdom of Louis the German were informed of the absolution and ordered to proclaim it to the faithful.[70]

Lothair had reached the turning of the road. Forsaken by the woman for whom he braved so much papal wrath and assured of Hadrian's willingness to grant

[68] *Ibid.*, 1237, 1263. After the death of Lothair the pope made unsuccessful attempts to prevent the invasion of his territories. A consequence of this failure was the treaty of Mersen in 870. *Ibid.*, 1291–95.

[69] *Ibid.*, 1265–66.   [70] *Ibid.*, 1266.

forgiveness if he manifested a respectable degree of penitence, he came to the Holy City in the early summer of 869. After visiting the tomb of the Apostles, he was received in audience by the pontiff. After he swore that he had observed the agreement he had made with Arsenius, the legate, and promised to abstain from sin in the future, he was forgiven by the pope. The reconciled monarch thereupon set out for home but died on the way at Placentia. His death was regarded by the chroniclers as an evidence of providential punishment for his sins and for swearing falsely that he had not violated his oath to Arsenius.[71]

The long struggle was thus brought to a dramatic close. It is quite true that "The history of the divorce of Teutberga . . . is a fair illustration of the manner in which [Nicholas] reduced to practice the theories of the 'False Decretals' and laid the foundations of that papal omnipotence which was to overshadow Christendom." [72] There is likewise little doubt but that the pope's labors during the tortuous course of the case enhanced the prestige of his office as the moral arbiter of Christian Europe. His attitude was a great step forward in the direction of inculcating in the minds of the clergy a conception of their duty to the Church which must take precedence over their obligations to any secular powers or to any ecclesiastical superiors not in sympathy with the policies of the Holy See.

The doctrine that "kings, in the event that they enunciate demands which are in contravention to the moral

---

[71] Hincmarus, *Annales*, in *M.G.H., SS.*, I, 482; Regino Prumiensis, *Chronicon*, in *M.G.H., SS.*, I, 580.

[72] H. C. Lea, *Studies in Church History* (Philadelphia, 1883), 159.

law, forfeit the right of obedience" [73] was a cardinal
feature of Nicholas' conception of the relationship between the Church and the secular power. It must not
be forgotten, however, that in addition to the undoubted
desire to assert the power of the Church over worldly
magnates as a means of enhancing the prestige of the
papacy, Nicholas was also conscious that "during all his
conflict . . . with the royal and with the episcopal
power, the moral and religious sympathies of mankind
could but be on his side . . . in the defence of the innocent and defenceless and in vindication of the sanctity
of marriage." [74]

[73] A. Greinacher, *Die Anschauungen des Papstes Nikolaus I über das
Verhältnis von Staat und Kirche* (Berlin, 1909), 47.
[74] H. Milman, *History of Latin Christianity* (London, 1883), II, 302.

Chapter V

ENFORCEMENT FROM NICHOLAS TO INNOCENT III

King Robert of France and Bertha

THE marital adventures of King Robert the Pious of France (996–1031) afford an interesting instance of papal enforcement of the marriage laws. Robert's first wife was Rozala, later called Susanna, daughter of Berengar, a claimant to the throne of Italy.[1] Rozala was first married to the Count of Flanders, but her husband died soon after the nuptials.[2] She then was married to young Robert, who, however, soon dismissed her because he considered her too old.[3] The marriage doubtless had been a political one, for it "raised the prestige of the King of France in Flanders and ended a struggle which had lasted almost half a century." [4]

The spurned wife endeavored to retaliate. She sought to recover her dower but was unable to secure it from the king. She then built a fortress in a commanding position at Montreuil, which had been part of her dower, in order to deny passage to Robert's boats. Some sympathy was excited for her, but for the most part it

---

[1] *Annales Elnonenses,* in *M.G.H., SS.,* V, 19.

[2] *Genealogiae Comitum Flandriae,* in *M.G.H., SS.,* IX, 306.

[3] Richerus, *Historiarum Libri IV, Société de l'histoire de France* (Paris, 1845), II, 270.

[4] C. Pfister, *Études sur le règne de Robert le Pieux* (Paris, 1885), 46.

was not openly expressed.[5] After vainly seeking to coerce Robert into a restitution of her dowry, she retired
to Flanders, where she died in 1003.[6]

Robert's next wife was Bertha, daughter of the King
of Burgundy, who had been recently bereft of her husband, Odo, Count of Blois.[7] There was also some consideration of political advantage involved in this marriage.[8]
Two impediments to the union existed. In the first
place, the couple were spiritual relatives, that is, Robert
had received a son of Bertha from the Sacred Font,
which made her his co-mother.[9] The couple were also
related within the third degree of blood relationship.[10]
Gerbert, Archbishop of Rheims, when asked to give his
permission for the marriage, refused, ostensibly on the
ground that the relationships precluded legitimate
canonical marriage.[11] The ceremony was performed
despite injunctions against it and probably took place
in 997, that is, shortly before Robert ascended the
throne.[12]

The chroniclers of the time were lavish in praise of
Robert's learning and piety. He was described as a "man
of excellent honesty and great piety, the ornament of
clerks, the nourisher of monks, the father of the poor,

[5] Richerus, *Historiarum, Soc. hist. Fr.*, II, 270.

[6] *Annales Elnonenses*, in *M.G.H., SS.*, V, 19.

[7] Richerus, *Historiarum, Soc. hist. Fr.*, II, 281.

[8] *Rythmus Satyricus de Temporibus Roberti Regis*, in *Recueil des historiens des Gaules et de la France* (ed. Bouquet, Paris, 1900–1904), X, 94.

[9] *Historiae Francicae Fragmentum*, in *R.H.F.*, X, 211.

[10] Pfister, *Études sur le règne de Robert le Pieux*, 49.

[11] Richerus, *Historiarum, Soc. hist. Fr.*, II, 308.

[12] J. Mabillon (ed.), *Annales Ordinis Sancti Benedicti* (Paris, 1703), IV, 96, 106.

the assiduous servitor of the true God, a king not only of peoples but even of their morals." [13] He was also reputed to be "distinguished in the perfection of all knowledge." [14] In addition, he was "more than superficially taught in the church songs," several of which he composed.[15] During his boyhood he had been a pupil of the famous scholar, Archbishop Gerbert, who soon was to crown his distinguished career by becoming Pope Sylvester II (999–1003).[16]

By his marriage to Bertha, no matter how pious he may have been in other respects, Robert undoubtedly committed a palpable violation of the church law. The fact that the pope at the time was Gregory V (996–999), noted for his reforming zeal, made it almost inevitable that an attempt would be made to discipline such a prominent offender.

The marriage case was, to some degree, coupled with another matter that had given acute displeasure to the Holy See. In a synod convoked by Hugh Capet in 991, Archbishop Arnulf of Rheims had been deposed ostensibly on the grounds that "according to the canons, one born of a concubine ought not to be made a bishop." [17] Actually, however, the deposition had been a punishment for the support which Arnulf had given Charles of Lorraine, a rival for the crown.[18] The deposed prel-

---

[13] Ademarus, *Chronica*, in *Collection des textes pour servir à l'étude et à l'enseignement de l'histoire*, XX, 154.

[14] Helgaldus Floriacensis, *Vita Roberti Regis*, in *R.H.F.*, X, 99.

[15] *Chronica Albici Monachi Trium Fontium*, in *M.G.H., SS.*, XXIII, 776.

[16] Helgaldus Floriacensis, *Vita Roberti Regis*, in *R.H.F.*, X, 99; *Chronica Albici Monachi Trium Fontium*, in *M.G.H., SS.*, XXIII, 776.

[17] Ordericus Vitalis, *Ecclesiastica Historia*, Soc. hist. Fr., II, Pt. I, 172.

[18] Richerus, *Historiarum*, Soc. hist. Fr., II, 308.

ate had been imprisoned, and Gerbert was elected in his stead.[19]

The pope's first action in regard to the affairs of the Frankish kingdom was the convocation of the Synod of Pavia in the year 997, wherein it was decreed that "all western bishops who were implicated in the deposition of the archbishop . . . are suspended from the episcopal office." Bishop Adelbero, who was held especially responsible for the illegal action, was permanently degraded.[20] It was also decreed in the same synod that "King Robert, who took to wife his relative, against the apostolic prohibition, be called to satisfaction, together with the bishops consenting to this marriage. If they refuse, they are to be deprived of communion." [21]

Abbo, the abbot of Cluny, was sent from Rome by the pope late in the same year. He was ordered to take measures to enforce the separation of Robert and Bertha and to secure the restoration of Arnulf.[22] Soon after his arrival in France, Abbo reported to the pope: "I derived the sense of your soul faithfully and simply as you ordered; nor did I fear the animosity of the king; but I kept the faith which I promised you, indeed, I added nothing, withdrew nothing, and abandoned nothing." He reported that Arnulf had been reinstated, but in regard to Robert his answer was vague. He declared that, "witness, indeed, my Lord Robert, brilliant king of the French who is called a spiritual son, ordered to make satisfaction to you and so to the Blessed Peter, Prince

[19] Ordericus Vitalis, *Ecclesiastica Historia, Soc. hist. Fr.,* II, Pt. I, 172; Richerus, *Historiarum, Soc. hist. Fr.,* II, 273, 275.

[20] *M.G.H., SS.,* III, 694.   [21] *Ibid.*

[22] *Vita Sancti Abbonis,* in Migne, *P.L.,* CXXXIX, 394 ff.; *Epistolae Sancti Abbonis,* in *R.H.F.,* X, 435–36.

of the Apostles, whose functions you now carry out in the world." [23]

The pope apparently understood Abbo's letter to mean that the king had proved amenable to suasion, for in replying to his letter he wrote, "I refer thanks for your benevolence to me, seeking that you direct brother R. to our presence, who will inform us concerning your prosperity and concerning the promise of the king." [24]

The Holy See was soon disillusioned, but the Crescentian troubles at Rome apparently impeded the application of coercive measures.[25] However, toward the end of 998 a council assembled at Rome, which pronounced a sentence of anathema upon Robert if he did not at once separate from Bertha and do seven years penance for his sin.[26]

The king failed to sever the illicit union, for a charter of October, 999, bears the joint names of the king and of Queen Bertha.[27] His recalcitrance automatically subjected him to the pains of anathema, although it is not known just when and under what circumstances the sentence was definitely pronounced. There is also some slight reason to suppose that an interdict was laid, for a historian of the time declared that the queen was "a co-mother of the king, that is, the king had received her son from the Sacred Font. But Pope Gregory learning of this, struck all France by anathema." [28]

The termination of the case came with the capitula-

---

[23] *R.H.F.*, X, 431.   [24] *Ibid.*
[25] Thietmarus, *Chronicon*, in *M.G.H.*, *SS.*, III, 776–77.
[26] Hefele, *Conciliengeschichte*, IV, 653; Mansi, *Sacrorum Conciliorum Collectio*, XIX, 223.
[27] *Historiae Francicae Fragmentum*, in *R.H.F.*, X, 211.
[28] Helgaldus Floriacensis, *Vita Roberti Regis*, in *R.H.F.*, X, 107.

tion of the king, who finally relinquished the woman.
We cannot, with assurance, assign a reason for his change
of heart. Helgaldus, his biographer and apologist, answered critics of the king's conduct by comparing him
with David, who had sinned in a like manner and who
had, in addition, greatly aggravated his guilt by procuring the death of the husband of the woman whom he
coveted. David's sins had been forgiven because, in true
contrition, he performed adequate penance. In a like
manner, Robert, experiencing a change of heart, "after
the confession of his guilt, prayed for mercy, deplored
the calamity, fasted, prayed, and transmitted the testimony of his confession by publishing it to the world in
perpetual sorrow." [29]

There is another interesting and not impossible version. An unknown historian informs us that "the king,
held by a love more than just for the woman, on no
account wished to dismiss her until the Omnipotent
Himself endeavored to correct him. Then, indeed, the
woman conceived by the said king, but instead of bringing forth a son, bore a monster, which event frightened
the king and compelled him to repudiate the woman.
This being done, he deserved to be absolved with his
whole kingdom." [30] It is possible that the queen had a
miscarriage and that the incompletely developed fetus
was regarded as a monster sent by providential intervention. Contrition, especially in one of indubitably
pious temperament, was doubtless a powerful motive in
inducing the king to acquiesce in the demands of the

[29] *Ibid.*
[30] *Historiae Francicae Fragmentum,* in *R.H.F.,* X, 211.

Church, while failure to bear an heir may have played its part in bringing about the separation.[31]

ENFORCEMENT OF THE LAW BY GREGORY VII
(1073–1086)

Gregory VII intervened in a number of interesting marital cases involving the enforcement of the law precluding marriages among relatives. In April, 1073, he took action in a case at Florence. A woman of that city had married a relative by blood, and upon his decease she recovered her dowry and retained the marriage gifts. She then desired to contract another marriage, "whereas this rascality which she committed should have made her smart in perpetuity." The pope ordered the Bishop of Florence to determine the exact degree of relationship that had existed between the woman and her former husband by interrogating the oldest residents of the town. If the report of kinship were confirmed by investigation, the bishop was directed to quash all legal instruments relating to dower and gifts so that the errant woman might not derive material profit from her sin.[32]

In September of 1074 Gregory wrote a letter of commendation to William, Count of Poitiers, who voluntarily had separated from his wife when he learned that consanguinity, in a degree sufficiently close to preclude valid marriage, existed between them. The pope expressed his appreciation of the magnitude of the sacrifice which the count had made and assured him that his

---

[31] Pfister, *Études sur le règne de Robert le Pieux*, 106.
[32] Jaffé, *Bibliotheca Rerum Germanicarum*, II, 13–14.

obedience would have its recompense. The pontiff rejoiced at the count's salvation from sin and the vindication of the honor of his family and admonished him on no account to live in the same house with his illicit wife pending final disposition of the case lest he be inveigled into abandonment of his salutary resolutions.[33]

Another case in which Gregory intervened concerned a sister of the Bishop of Pavia. It was reported to a Roman synod that this woman married the Marquis Azo, who was related to her within the proscribed degrees, and a rigorous examination of the case was ordered. The pope summoned the bishop and his brother-in-law, the marquis, to appear at Rome to present their side of the case.[34]

The bishop proved disobedient, for in a letter of September of the same year he was berated by the pope for his contumacy. He was ordered to appear at a synod, to be held in Rome during the following February, if he wished to be heard in behalf of his sister. The pontiff explained that the relationship existing between the couple in question had been proved by witnesses and oaths, but one more opportunity would be afforded the bishop to present a defense of the marriage before nullity was definitely decreed.[35]

At the same time the pope dispatched a letter to the wife, pointing out that he already had bound the marquis by oath to refrain from intercourse with her. He went on to say that "in behalf of the Blessed Peter, we order you to remove yourself entirely from his consort and cohabitation so that you may do penance for the iniquity perpetrated, in order to recover the grace of

[33] *Ibid.*, 109, 111.   [34] *Ibid.*, 76.   [35] *Ibid.*, 149.

God." Matilda also was informed that if she considered herself unjustly treated by the Holy See, she would have the opportunity to lodge an appeal before the next Roman synod. No defense was subsequently presented, and the annulment of the union therefore remained in effect.[36]

In February, 1079, Gregory wrote to Centullus, the count of Bearn, saying that he had received excellent reports of the count's conduct, for he was reputed to be a "lover of justice, a defender of the poor, and a disseminator of peace." However, he had committed one blameworthy act when he married his ward, who was also his blood relative. The pope directed that the marriage be dissolved at once lest because of this sin the count "lose his soul and ruin the noble woman under his care." [37]

In the case of the Marquis of Bonifacio, who married his brother's widow, the pope adopted a much severer attitude. He ordered his legates to warn the marquis to separate from the woman and instructed them to excommunicate him if he refused to comply with their directions.[38]

PHILIP I OF FRANCE AND BERTRADE

The marital affairs of King Philip (1060–1108) engendered a struggle with the papacy of long continuance and varying fortune. Philip first was married to Bertha sometime before 1075, and he had at least two children by her, a son, Louis, and a daughter.[39] For some un-

---

[36] E. Caspar (ed.), *Gregorii VII Registrum* (Berlin, 1907), I, 172.
[37] Jaffé, *Bibliotheca Rerum Germanicarum*, II, 357.
[38] *Ibid.*, 390.
[39] Hariulfus, *Vita Beati Arnulfi*, in *R.H.F.*, XIV, 56; XVI, xxx.

known reason he finally desired separation from his wife. A claim of relationship was brought forward by the king with the result that a subservient synod pronounced a sentence nullifying the marriage.[40] The repudiation probably took place in the year 1092.[41] There is no account of the proceedings extant, but a description of a later synod, wherein Louis VII was separated from his wife, Eleanor, gives us a fairly accurate idea of the probable proceedings in the case of Philip and Bertha.[42] Witnesses presumably were heard who made depositions alleging kinship between the parties, whereupon the assembled churchmen, after due consideration, pronounced the union void.

The king then began to look about for a new bride. He asked the aid and advice of Bishop Ivo of Chartres, who refused to help him because he considered the repudiation of Bertha illegal.[43] Philip endeavored to overcome the objections of Ivo by asserting that he had procured pontifical authority for the annulment of his marriage, but Ivo placed no credence in these allegations.[44] It is indeed possible that the king sincerely believed he had proceeded regularly by obtaining the assurance of the clergy in his entourage that everything had been conducted in a canonical manner.

Before the end of 1092 the royal quest for a new wife was ended; the object of the king's affections was Bertrade, sister of the Count of Montfort.[45] There were

---

[40] *De Gestis Francorum,* in *R.H.F.,* XII, 122.

[41] Petrus Vivus Senonensis, *Chronica,* in *R.H.F.,* XII, 280.

[42] *Historia Gloriosi Regis Ludovici VII, Coll. des textes,* IV, 19, 32, 163.

[43] *R.H.F.,* XV, 73–74.   [44] *Ibid.*

[45] Petrus Vivus Senonensis, *Chronica,* in *R.H.F.,* XII, 280.

most serious impediments to such a union. Bertrade was the wife of Count Fulk of Anjou, a vassal of Philip, and marriage with her would be a palpable violation of the ecclesiastical marital law as well as a transgression of feudal custom.[46] Fulk's second wife had been Ermengarde, who was related to him within the forbidden degrees, with the result that he had been excommunicated by Gregory VII and ordered to separate from her.[47] He finally submitted so that he was left free to contract with Bertrade, and their union seems to have been legal in all respects. Fulk, moreover, was related to Philip in the third degree of blood relationship, which made his wife a relative of the king in the third degree of affinity of the first "kind." [48]

The accounts of Philip's union with Bertrade are divergent. According to one version, the king "carried off the wife of Fulk, Count of Anjou." [49] Another account records that "the wicked Philip came to Tours, and speaking with the wife of Fulk of Anjou, persuaded her to become queen. . . . That sinful woman, having left her husband, on the following night followed the king, who left soldiers at Maundraio near the bridge of Bevronis, and these soldiers led her to Orléans. There the most lustful king garnished her home by rascally nuptials." [50]

Ordericus stated that Bertrade, "fearing lest her husband do to her as he had done to two others and cause her to be exposed to the contempt of all like a vile har-

[46] R.H.F., XIII, 625.
[47] Jaffé, Bibliotheca Rerum Germanicarum, II, 498.
[48] R.H.F., XIII, 625; XVI, 42–43.
[49] Chronicon Turonensis, in R.H.F., XII, 465.
[50] Gesta Consulum Andegavensium, in R.H.F., XII, 499.

lot, and knowing of the king's nobility and beauty, sent a most faithful emissary to King Philip of the Franks. She preferred, indeed, to leave her spouse and seek another rather than be left by her husband, open to the scorn of all." Philip, "the tender prince," was touched by her adversity and easily was induced to acquiesce in her wishes.[51]

It is hardly likely that Philip carried off Bertrade without at least her passive connivance.[52] Even though she were a willing captive, the king's guilt in adhering to a married woman who was in addition his relative was in no way mitigated.

Philip attempted to secure the approval of his new union by the clergy of his realm but found that "no bishop of all the Franks was ready to perform that execrable consecration; but all, standing on the rigor of ecclesiastical righteousness, tried to please God more than man and were prepared that the evil union be unanimously detested by anathema." [53] Ivo of Chartres strenuously opposed the king's marital project and was thrown into prison for his pains.[54] In a plaintive letter to the king he declared that "since you are exasperated because of the helpful warnings which I directed to your Serenity, animated by the highest fidelity and charity, you distrusted me, and, having seized the goods of the episcopal house, you exposed me to my adversaries, and I am laden with great and heavy vexation." [55]

---

[51] Ordericus Vitalis, *Ecclesiastica Historia*, Soc. hist. Fr., II, Pt. III, 386.

[52] *Epistolae Urbani II Papae*, in *R.H.F.*, XIV, 702.

[53] Ordericus Vitalis, *Ecclesiastica Historia*, Soc. hist. Fr., II, Pt. III, 387.

[54] *R.H.F.*, XIV, 702.   [55] *Ibid.*, XV, 78.

Some time later, either because of persuasion or co-ercion, the marriage finally was given episcopal sanction. Ordericus declared that Odo, Bishop of Bayeaux, was the prelate who approved the union.[56] Pope Urban II, however, accused the Bishop of Senlis.[57]

In writing to the Archbishop of Rheims, the pope declared that "you, indeed, dear brother Rainald, especially brought about this evil because the Bishop of Senlis, who, as we hear, confirmed this crime of public adultery by his consent, is subject to you." The pope declared that "if you had exercised the priestly office which you fill with the required consideration, then that evil infamy would not have arrived to our ears unpunished." "For what reason, we wonder," chided the pontiff, "could you tolerate that a king of a brilliant realm left his wife irregularly and joined in marriage in nefarious love with his relative, oblivious of human shame, heedless of divine fear, against law, against legal and canonical sanction, against the customs of the whole Church." Failure to protest energetically was tantamount to acquiescence, in the opinion of the pope. The archbishop was ordered to endeavor to persuade the king to relinquish his illicit mate, but if he did not prove amenable to mild measures, ecclesiastical censures were to be utilized. Moreover, if Ivo of Chartres were not immediately released, Philip's kingdom was to be subjected to an interdict without further orders from the Holy See.[58]

Ivo was released in October, 1092, partly because of

---

[56] Ordericus Vitalis, *Ecclesiastica Historia, Soc. hist. Fr.*, II, Pt. III, 387.

[57] *R.H.F.*, XIV, 702–703.   [58] *Ibid.*

assistance of the archbishops and partly because of the
co-operation of the Bishop of Le Mans, to whom he
ascribed the major credit for his release. Philip, however, did not cease his persecution of Ivo after his release.[59] No restitution was made for the damages done
to his property, and he was vexed by citations before the
king's court.[60] Ivo finally decided to inform the pope
more fully regarding his mistreatment and went to
Rome for that purpose in November, 1092.[61]

Upon his return from the Holy City in January,
1093, Wido, the royal chamberlain, endeavored to reconcile Philip with the prelate by his mediation. Ivo expressed his gratitude for these efforts but held out little
hope that they would prove successful. He privately
informed Wido that sterner measures were imminent,
for during his sojourn at Rome he had seen the letters
which Urban had prepared to send to all the French
clergy ordering the application of ecclesiastical censures.
The letters had just arrived in France, but Ivo declared
that "for the love of the king, I caused them to be
withheld, because I do not wish to move against his
kingdom for any reason." The chamberlain was asked to
inform the king privately as to what measures were
pending, in a last attempt to induce him to amend his
conduct without the application of coercion.[62]

The breach between the king and Ivo was accentuated by the prelate's refusal to furnish a military contingent. He held fiefs from the king who needed troops
to aid Robert of Normandy against King William Rufus
of England.[63] Ivo justified his position largely on the

---

[59] *Ibid.*, XV, 78.   [60] *Ibid.*   [61] *Ibid.*, 80.
[62] *Ibid.*, 78.   [63] *Ibid.*, 82.

ground that the king by his sins had forfeited the claim to the services of his vassals.

The next stage in the case was the call issued by Hugh, Archbishop of Lyons, the resident papal legate, for a synod to be held in October, 1094. The legate declared that he had been ordered by the pope to convoke such an assembly to deal with the matter of the king's marriage, but he had been reluctant to assume the burden and had deferred his compliance so long that further delay would be considered tantamount to disobedience.[64] Philip countered by summoning a council to meet at Rheims in September of 1094.[65] Prestige was gained for the royal assembly by inducing the Archbishop of Sens to attend and act in collaboration with the Archbishop of Rheims. The acts of this council have been lost, but it seems that accusations were heard against Ivo of Chartres.[66]

In October the legatine synod assembled at Autun. "In this synod King Philip of the Gauls was excommunicated because of his having espoused another woman with his legitimate wife still living." [67] The separation of Philip from his first wife apparently was impugned as well as his union with Bertrade.

Philip appealed the synod's decision and sent an embassy to Rome to secure annulment of the sentence. It was represented to the pope that great disaffection existed among the French clergy because of the treatment of the king, and their withdrawal from obedience to the Holy See was threatened. Ivo, however, urged the pope

[64] *Ibid.*, 791.   [65] *Ibid.*, XIV, 750.
[66] *Senonensis Chronographus Clarius*, in *R.H.F.*, XII, 280.
[67] Bertholdus Constantiensis, *Chronica*, in *R.H.F.*, XIV, 680.

not to be deceived by those "through whose mouths the spirit of lies speaks," and advised that he refuse to be intimidated "even though they say that the ax will be laid to the root of the tree unless you relax the law or suspend the sword." [68]

An assembly of the French clergy then was held at Troyes apparently to hear the pope's response to the embassy of Philip. The king tentatively agreed to alter his conduct, for, according to Ivo, he "promised to do much good and eschew much evil if he might retain for a time the woman whom he held illicitly, with the peace of the Apostolic See and the ecclesiastical communion." Ivo was not to be placated by such a partial concession and informed the king that "no one can wipe out his sin by redemption or commutation as long as he wishes to remain in it." [69]

At the Council of Placentia in 1095 it was anticipated that some disposition would be made of Philip's case, but the king, after having begun the journey to attend the meeting, was delayed, and his excuses were deemed sufficient to justify a postponement. [70]

The next stage in the struggle was the action taken at the Council of Clermont, held in November, 1095, at which Urban II preached his famous sermon summoning Europe to the First Crusade. We are informed that "Urban, in his council, overflowed with authority so that, indeed, with constancy, he excommunicated Philip, King of the Franks, who copulated with Bertrade, the wife of the Count of Anjou, after he had left his own wife." The pope in pronouncing sentence paid no heed to a considerable sentiment in favor of the king

---

[68] *R.H.F.*, XV, 84.   [69] *Ibid.*, 85.   [70] *Ibid.*, 81.

that had arisen among the local clergy, for, as Gilbert tells us, "he disregarded the intercessions of many influential persons and the offers of many rewards, and he did not fear to tarry for a time within the borders of the king's realm." [71]

Shortly after the adjournment of this council another was convoked at Tours to deal with the French clergy, who insisted that the king be absolved and, indeed, even ventured to accord absolution on their own initiative. Urban demanded that the sentence of excommunication be observed and held that no absolution could be granted without the consent of the Holy See.[72]

The king finally made his submission at the Council of Nîmes shortly after Easter, 1096. Philip "humbly came to offer satisfaction, and, having repudiated the adultress, he was received in grace and showed himself sufficiently prompt in the service of the lord pope." [73] Urban himself presided on this occasion, for the chronicler stated that "Urban returned to Saintes and celebrated Easter there. Then he set out for Rome, and on his way back again to Nîmes he held a council there and reconciled Philip, king of the Franks." [74]

The penitent king did not long persist in his good resolutions. Late in 1097 he again was excommunicated by the Archbishop of Lyons, acting in his capacity of papal legate.[75] Ivo of Chartres considered himself in jeopardy and asked that his resignation be accepted since, as he declared, "I cannot refrain from giving my

---

[71] Gilbertus Montensis, *Chronica*, in *M.G.H.*, *SS.*, XXI, 503.
[72] *R.H.F.*, XIV, 722.
[73] Bertholdus Constantiensis, *Chronica*, in *R.H.F.*, XIV, 685.
[74] *Chronicon Malleacensi*, in *R.H.F.*, XII, 403.
[75] *R.H.F.*, XV, 96, 98, 100.

resignation before I encounter anew the enmity of the king for the same cause as before." [76]

Absolution from this second excommunication was accorded by Urban early in 1098. The pontiff informed the French clergy that "a legate of our most dear son, Philip, King of the Franks, coming to us, bore words of humility and devotion and made satisfaction to us concerning the guilt of the woman for which our venerable colleague inflicted on him the sentence of interdict." [77] The royal emissary affirmed that the king had not had any intercourse with Bertrade since his absolution at Nîmes, and the pope, after directing that some of the bishops of Philip's realm be sent to Rome to confirm the deposition of the legate, directed the French clergy to consider the king absolved. [78] The interdict seems to have been of the ambulatory form and does not appear to have been particularly effective. William of Malmsbury narrated that "while the king was in a town, divine services were not held, but after he left, the ringing of the bells resounded; whereupon he said, laughing like a fool, 'listen, bells, why do you pursue us?' " [79] There was some feeling that the pope had been too gullible in according absolution merely on the strength of the allegation of the king's emissary. [80]

The death of Urban II in July, 1099, left upon his successor, Paschal II (1099–1118), the burden of enforcing the papal policy with respect to the defiant king. The new pope lost little time in taking measures to secure observance of the mandates of his predecessor. He

[76] *Ibid.*, 100.   [77] *Ibid.*, XIV, 729.   [78] *Ibid.*
[79] Guillelmus Malmsburgensis, *Chronica, Rolls Series,* II, 480.
[80] Hugo Flaviniacensis, *Chronica,* in *M.G.H., SS.,* VIII, 474.

sent two legates into France, who, after consultation with Ivo of Chartres, convoked a council at Poitiers in November, 1100.[81]

Here anathema again was pronounced against Philip despite the strenuous efforts of the Count of Poitiers in his behalf. Apparently, there was some attempt to intimidate the assembled clergy by violence.[82] Armed retainers of the count menaced the prelates; indeed, according to one version, the count left the assembly in high dudgeon after the pronouncement of its sentence and threatened to follow the members after adjournment to do physical harm to them.[83] According to another account the townspeople surged into the assembly hall and mishandled the clergy; a third version stated that several of the more prominent ecclesiastics were flogged by the mob.[84] All accounts agree that there was some attempt at intimidation by violence or the threat of violence. This is additional evidence that the course of action taken by the papacy and the more strict French clergy evoked no inconsiderable opposition among clergy and laity alike. Philip, however, "was obdurate in his sin and scorned the exhortations of fatherly corrections like a deaf asp who closes his ears to the voice of incantation; and he lay sick, putrid in this adulterous sin." [85]

In the meantime the interdict continued in force. It was first formally laid by the Archbishop of Lyons in his capacity of legate, but it was raised soon after by

[81] *Vita Sancti Hilarii Pictavensis*, in *R.H.F.*, XIV, 104; XV, 104.
[82] *Ibid.*
[83] Hugo Flaviniacensis, *Chronica*, in *M.G.H.*, *SS.*, VIII, 493.
[84] *Ibid.*; *Vita Bernardi Tyronensis*, in *R.H.F.*, XIV, 169.
[85] Ordericus Vitalis, *Ecclesiastica Historia*, Soc. hist. Fr., II, Pt. III, 389.

Urban II. Apparently the anathema pronounced at Poitiers had the effect of restoring the ambulatory interdict, for Ordericus stated that "in whatever city or town the king came, as soon as this was heard by the clergy, all ringing of bells and songs of clerks ceased. Public distress was aroused and the cult of the Lord was privately exercised as long as the transgressor Prince delayed in this diocese." [86] Another report stated that "when the king tarried at Sens for twenty days all the churches in the whole town were closed." [87]

Two factors joined to bring about the final reconciliation of the king to the Church. In the first place, he began to be afflicted with sundry infirmities, which were, in medieval fashion, ascribed to providential intervention occasioned by his sin.[88] Secondly, the efforts of Bertrade to secure the succession of her children to the throne to the exclusion of Louis, Philip's son by his first wife, made Louis an inveterate enemy of the illicit queen, and he used all his influence with his father to secure her dismissal.[89]

In 1102 Ivo informed the pope that Philip was in a receptive mood for reconciliation and was contemplating dispatch of an embassy to Rome. He warned against a premature acceptance of the king's assurances lest the unfortunate experiences of the past be duplicated.[90] The papal legate, Richard, who had come into France early in 1102, was eager for peace. He summoned a council

---

[86] *Ibid.*

[87] Hugo Flaviniacensis, *Chronica*, in *M.G.H., SS.*, VIII, 498.

[88] Ordericus Vitalis, *Ecclesiastica Historia, Soc. hist. Fr.*, II, Pt. III, 389.

[89] *Ibid.*   [90] *R.H.F.*, XV, 116.

at Troyes to achieve an amicable settlement, but his efforts proved futile.[91]

The absolution finally came in August, 1104, at the
Synod of Beaugency in the diocese of Orléans. The king
and queen each took an oath to abjure all carnal intercourse, and even conversation between them was to be
foresworn unless carried on in the presence of persons
above suspicion. After some wrangling as to the proper
procedure in according absolution, the king was finally
released from the sentence.[92]

Paschal II in October wrote to the French clergy and
expressed his approval of their action.[93] An assembly
was convoked at Paris to hear the public proclamation
of the absolution. The pope's letter was read, and the
Bishops of Orléans and Paris asked the king if he wished
to conform to the terms agreed upon at the August assembly. The latter replied that "he wished to make satisfaction to God and to the Holy Roman Church, to
submit himself to the orders of the Apostolic See, and
to follow the counsel of the bishops there assembled."
Barefooted, the king knelt and promised to do penance
for his sin and was formally absolved. Both he and the
queen then took oaths promising henceforth to refrain
from all intercourse.[94]

The famous case had been finally brought to official
termination. There is, however, some reason to believe
that the separation was even yet not final and complete,
for in October, 1106, Philip was spoken of as being with
Queen Bertrade.[95] Nevertheless, if the king did not

---

[91] *Ibid.*, 128.   [92] *Ibid.*, 129.   [93] *Ibid.*, 29.
[94] *Ibid.*, 197.   [95] *Ibid.*, XII, 486 n.

totally relinquish the society of the woman for whom he apparently had great affection, his intercourse with her was not so open and flagrant as to cause any further protest from either the local clergy or the Holy See. The papal policy had been officially successful although the king's obedience could only be secured, after much delay and tergiversation, by the application of every ecclesiastical weapon in the garner of the Church. The popes had been inhibited in their efforts to enforce the marital law by the resistance, overt or passive, of a considerable portion of the French clergy, who proved themselves only too ready to acquiesce in the king's demands even when these entailed connivance with palpable violation of the church law. A great share in the burden of enforcing the law was borne by Bishop Ivo of Chartres, who proved himself willing to submit to oppression rather than condone any violation of the canons. Urban II, by his courage in dealing with the king within the borders of his own realm, and indeed in opposition to the wishes of many of the local clergy, undoubtedly did much to enhance papal prestige and to establish it as the ultimate source of worldly authority from which not even kings were immune.

Enforcement from the Pontificate of Paschal II (1099–1118) to the End of the Pontificate of Celestine III (1191–1198)

Paschal *ca.* 1110 ordered the Bishop of Compostello (Santiago) to dissolve the marriage contracted by the daughter of Alfonso, King of Castile. The pontiff declared that "Omnipotent God had established him to rule over His people so that he might correct their sins

and make known the wishes of God." The bishop was
admonished, therefore, "to correct with retribution the
crime of incest which had been perpetrated by the
daughter of the king . . . so that she would either desist from that presumption or be deprived of the society
of the Church as well as of secular power." [96]

The same pontiff was called upon to issue a decretal
against incestuous marriages which were being contracted throughout Spain and some parts of France as
a kind of penance for the sins of the parents of the
parties. The pope proclaimed that such marriages were
to be straightway annulled, and strict prohibitions were
issued to prevent a recurrence of the abuse.[97]

Calixtus II (1119–1124) in 1121 ordered the dissolution of a marriage in Castile on the ground that the
man had enjoyed carnal intercourse with a relative of
his wife prior to their marriage.[98] Celestine II (1143–
1144), Lucius II (1144–1145), and Eugenius III
(1145–1153) intervened in several minor marital cases
involving relationship to exercise the right of evocation
of the cases before the Holy See or to facilitate their
disposition by the local clergy.[99]

During the pontificate of Alexander III a considerable number of cases of the type under discussion arose
and made necessary papal intervention. In one case the
Bishop of Exeter was ordered to institute proceedings
in regard to Hugh of Kalega and his wife, who were alleged to be joined within the forbidden degrees. The
bishop directed to examine the testimony of witnesses
was exhorted to proceed with great caution since "it was

[96] Migne, *P.L.*, CLXIII, 280.　　[97] *Ibid.*, 134.
[98] *Ibid.*, 1211.　　[99] *R.H.F.*, XV, 409, 414, 426.

more tolerable, indeed, to allow some to be joined against the statutes of man than to separate, against the statutes of the Lord, those legitimately joined." [100]

The same bishop was the papal representative in another interesting case. A certain man in his diocese, after having had carnal intercourse with a woman, married her cousin "with reckless daring." The pope equivocated in his enforcement of the law. He directed that the marriage should be nullified and penance enjoined in case the previous relations of the man with his wife's relative were a matter of common knowledge. If, however, the sin had been kept secret, the bishop was directed to allow the marriage to continue, but penance was to be performed by the guilty man. [101]

In another instance a man betrothed to a woman with observance of all due forms subsequently had intercourse with the daughter of his promised bride. The pope decided that if the man had carnally known his betrothed prior to the public declaration of their engagement, he was to be compelled to marry her. If, on the other hand, there had been no carnal union, he was to marry the daughter unless it were established that he had entered upon illicit relations with her under the coercion of his father. [102]

A similar case arose in the diocese of Hereford. A certain A betrothed to a girl who was below the marriageable age, subsequently married her mother. The pope held that if he married the mother before the daughter attained the age of seven, the marriage was not to be nullified since no legal betrothal could be con-

[100] Mansi, *Sacrorum Conciliorum Collectio*, XXII, 311.
[101] *Ibid.*, 325–26.   [102] *Ibid.*, 307.

tracted with a girl who was below that age. However, if the marriage to the mother took place after her daughter reached the age necessary for legal betrothal, the union was to be dissolved, and the man was not to contract with either mother or daughter.[103]

Another interesting case arose in the diocese of Wighorn. A man repudiated his legitimate wife and married another who was alleged to be related to her in the second degree. An inquiry was ordered, and Alexander directed that if it were established that the two women were related within that degree, the second marriage was to be dissolved, and the guilty man was to remain continent. If, however, no kinship existed, he was to be compelled to return to his first wife and treat her with the required marital affection.[104]

The pope also was required to take cognizance of a case where a woman, after being legitimately married, was said to have slept nude with a relative of her husband, and "it was believed with the intention that he join carnally with her." Dissolution of the marriage was ordered, and permission was given to the outraged husband to contract a new marriage upon the death of his wife.[105]

Perhaps the strangest case of all that arose during Alexander's pontificate was the one in which the circumstances were as follows: A man concluded a legitimate marriage, but by the arguments and importunities of the girl's father he was prevailed upon to defer consummation of the union for more than a month. In the interim the bride's father, perhaps regretting the marriage and desiring to have it annulled, compelled his own wife to enter the bed of the hitherto continent bridegroom, whereupon he, "by the suggestion of the devil," enjoyed coition with her. The father again changed his mind, for soon after he insisted that the man consummate his legal marriage with the daughter, but the bridegroom refused until he could secure proper ecclesiastical permission. The case finally was examined by the pope, who ordered that if the sin with the mother had been committed before the marriage to her daughter had been consummated, the man was to do penance and remain with his legitimate wife. The rascally father was enjoined to keep secret the relations of the young man with the mother of his bride so that no scandal would arise from the sordid affair.[106]

Clement III dealt with two significant cases wherein consanguinity was admitted by the parties to marriages in order to procure dissolution of unions that had become distasteful. In one case a certain Count William allowed himself to be separated from his wife allegedly because of kinship, although he knew that no relationship existed between them and could have proved this fact had he so desired. After a time he contracted a second marriage, but his conscience troubled him because of his chicanery in regard to his first spouse. He thereupon confessed his sin and asked the bishop's advice. The puzzled prelate submitted the case to the pope for adjudication and was informed that the second marriage

---

[106] *Decretales Gregorii IX Papae,* Lib. IV, Tit. XII, c. 2. For other cases see *R.H.F.,* XV, 902; Migne, *P.L.,* CC, 852, 1092, 1280; A. Potthast, *Regesta Pontificum Romanorum* (Berlin, 1875), Nos. 10641, 11288, 11527, 11542, 11690, 13162, 13163, 13790, 13887, 13907, 13947, 14101, 14124.

was not to be dissolved, but penance was to be imposed on the guilty man. Also, in copulating with his wife, William was ordered to approach her "contritely" and with "condign sadness and reluctance." [107]

In the second case, a knight who was married for twenty-five years confessed that he was related to his wife within the forbidden degrees in order that he might be separated from her. The pontiff decided that the long continuance of the union was sufficient proof of its legality and quashed all proceedings for voiding it.[108]

Celestine III issued decisions in several cases. A certain G, after the death of his first wife, entered upon carnal relations with his stepdaughter. He subsequently remarried but continued his illicit relations "like a dog returning to his vomit." The pope decided that the second marriage was not to be dissolved, but he ordered that the guilty man "shall not know his wife as long as she lives, unless required by her to do so, and then he shall not approach her without grave sadness of heart." [109]

In ordering an examination of a case involving consanguinity, Celestine declared that "since from the assumption of the office of universal rule we are held to conduct the care of the safety of the flock committed to us, it beseems us to be especially cautious and careful concerning marriages, since, from them, if they are indiscreetly carried out, great perils to souls can result; that is, if those whom God joined are separated by man without reason, or conversely, are given leave mutually

---

[107] Migne, *P.L.*, CCIV, 1485.   [108] *Ibid.*, 1484.
[109] *Decretales Gregorii IX Papae*, Lib. IV, Tit. XII, c. 4.

to cohabit when it is established that they are joined by man against the will of God." [110]

Celestine also began action in two famous cases involving kings, but the chief burden of enforcing the law fell upon the shoulders of his successor, Innocent III.

[110] Migne, *P.L.*, CCVI, 1080.

CHAPTER VI

THE CASE OF PHILIP AUGUSTUS AND INGEBURG

A MOST important case of papal intervention in marital affairs was that occasioned by the marriage of Philip Augustus (1180–1223) with Ingeburg and the repudiation of the bride which immediately followed.

Soon after the death of his first wife, Elizabeth of Flanders, Philip sent an embassy, headed by Bishop Stephen of Noyon, to King Canute VI of Denmark asking for the hand of his sister, Ingeburg.[1] The emissaries were honorably received by the Danish sovereign, who evinced pleasure at the prospective nuptials.[2] Negotiations proceeded with dispatch until the matter of the dowry was reached. The French envoys asked that Canute, in consideration of his claims on England, attack that realm, but the king demurred, alleging that he had no quarrel with the English and that his small forces would be unable to cope with their renowned warriors.[3] A dower of ten thousand marks then was suggested, to which proposal Canute acquiesced after

---

[1] *Gesta Innocentii Tercii*, in Migne, *P.L.*, CCXIV, col. XLVIII; Rigordus, *Gesta Philippi Augusti*, Soc. hist. Fr., II, 38; Guillelmus Armoricus, *Gesta Philippi Augusti*, Soc. hist. Fr., II, 195; Guillelmus Neubrigensis, *Historia Anglicana*, R.S., I, 368.

[2] Rigordus, *Gesta Philippi Augusti*, Soc. hist. Fr., II, 124; Guillelmus Neubrigensis, *Historia Anglicana*, R.S., I, 368.

[3] Guillelmus Neubrigensis, *Historia Anglicana*, R.S., I, 368–69.

some consultation with his advisers.[4] There also was
apparently an understanding that Canute would aid
France with a naval force in a projected expedition
against England.[5]

The betrothal thus arranged, Canute sent Ingeburg,
"his most beautiful sister, a pious girl adorned with
good manners," [6] to her prospective husband. She was
escorted by a delegation headed by Peter, Bishop of
Rothschild. The party arrived at Amiens on August 14,
1193.[7] There Philip, consumed by impatience, awaited
her, and the marital ceremony was begun in the presence of bishops and secular magnates.[8] On the following
day Ingeburg was crowned "with the regal diadem, in
the sight of the whole town," [9] by the Archbishop of
Rheims.[10] But "marvelous to behold, on the same day,
the king, instigated by the devil and vexed by the sor-
ceries of evil, began to hate the wife so long desired." [11]
During the coronation, "by suggestion of the evil one,
he began vehemently to be horrified and to tremble and
pale at the sight of her so that, very much perturbed,
he sustained himself with difficulty until the end of the
ceremony." [12] The king wished to be separated from his
wife at once but was induced to endeavor to consummate the marriage, in which attempt he alleged that he

---

[4] *R.H.F.*, XIX, 310.

[5] Roger de Hoveden, *Chronica*, R.S., III, 224–25.   [6] *Ibid.*

[7] *Gesta Innocentii Tercii*, in Migne, *P.L.*, CCXIV, col. XLVIII.

[8] *Ibid.;* Guillelmus Armoricus, *Gesta Philippi Augusti*, Soc. hist. Fr.,
II, 195.

[9] *Annales Aquicinctensis*, in *R.H.F.*, XVIII, 546.

[10] *Ibid.; Gesta Innocentii Tercii*, in Migne, *P.L.*, CCXIV, col.
XLVIII.

[11] Rigordus, *Gesta Philippi Augusti*, Soc. hist. Fr., II, 124–25.

[12] *Gesta Innocentii Tercii*, in Migne, *P.L.*, CCXIV, col. XLVIII.

failed.[13] He then hated his wife more than ever, forbidding anyone to mention her name.[14]

The cause of Philip's sudden aversion for his wife will perhaps forever remain a mystery. The writers of the time ascribed the phenomenon to diabolical machinations, with the exception of William of Newburgh, who declared that the "cause of this shameful levity is variously described, some say because of the fetid smell of the breath, others, that it was because of ugliness that he repudiated her, and others because he did not find her a virgin." [15] Of the modern writers Hurter [16] thinks that Philip's disgust during the ceremony was occasioned by contemplation of the failure of his plans against England, and this view is substantially the same as that held by Geraud.[17] Davidsohn,[18] however, while attempting no definite explanation inclines to the view that corporeal grounds were primarily responsible for the bride's repudiation.

Ardently desirous of ridding himself of his wife, Philip first wished to remand her to the custody of the Danish legates for escort back to Denmark, but the queen demurred.[19] The king then took counsel with his advisers, ecclesiastical and lay, and decided to seek nulli-

---

[13] Migne, *P.L.*, CCXV, 1494.

[14] *Gesta Innocentii Tercii*, in Migne, *P.L.*, CCXIV, col. XLVIII.

[15] Guillelmus Neubrigensis, *Historia Anglicana*, *R.S.*, I, 369.

[16] F. Hurter, *Geschichte Papst Innocenz des Dritten* (Hamburg, 1834), I, 170.

[17] *Bibliothèque de l'école des chartes* (1884), 10.

[18] R. Davidsohn, *Philip II, August von Frankreich und Ingeburg* (Stuttgart, 1888), 35.

[19] Roger de Hoveden, *Chronica*, *R.S.*, III, 224; Rigordus, *Gesta Philippi Augusti*, Soc. hist. Fr., II, 125; Radulphus de Diceto, *Ymagines Historiarum*, *R.S.*, II, 111.

fication of the marriage on the grounds of relationship. On November 4 an assembly was convoked at Compiègne.[20] A line of relationship was computed between Ingeburg and Elizabeth of Flanders, through Charles, Count of Flanders, which made Philip and Ingeburg relatives within the forbidden degrees of affinity.[21] Sixteen prominent ecclesiastics and lay nobles swore to this relationship, and on the basis of their depositions the Archbishop of Rheims, who presided at the council, declared the marriage dissolved.[22] Ingeburg was present at the council, but because of her ignorance of the French language she could take no effective part in the proceedings.[23] With the pronouncement of the sentence she ejaculated, *"Mala Francia, Mala Francia, Roma, Roma,"* thus signifying her intention to appeal to the pope.[24] After the annulment the queen was remanded to a monastery,[25] where "she was to keep continent and serve with prayers for the whole term of her life."[26] Although William le Breton assures us that "she received the necessities of life from the treasury,"[27] her supplies were unbecomingly meager as a letter of her friend, Stephen of Tournai, to the Archbishop of Rheims testified.[28]

[20] *Annales Aquicinctensis*, in *R.H.F.*, XVIII, 546.

[21] Davidsohn, *Philip II und Ingeburg*, 42, Anhang I.

[22] *Annales Aquicinctensis*, in *R.H.F.*, XVIII, 546.

[23] *Gesta Innocentii Tercii*, in Migne, *P.L.*, CCXIV, col. XLIX; Guillelmus Armoricus, *Gesta Philippi Augusti*, Soc. hist. Fr., II, 195; Roger de Hoveden, *Chronica*, R.S., III, 224.

[24] Roger de Hoveden, *Chronica*, R.S., III, 224.

[25] Davidsohn, *Philip II und Ingeburg*, 47.

[26] Rigordus, *Gesta Philippi Augusti*, Soc. hist. Fr., II, 125.

[27] Guillelmus Armoricus, *Gesta Philippi Augusti*, Soc. hist. Fr., II, 195.

[28] *Epistolae Stephani Tornacensis*, in Migne, *P.L.*, CCXI, No. 262.

Stimulated by Philip's efforts to secure a new bride,[29] protests began to be directed to Pope Celestine III. Canute, through William the Abbot, who had taken such a prominent part in the negotiations for the marriage, wrote to the pope declaring that the charges of affinity were false.[30] A genealogy was transmitted to the pontiff, maintaining, and apparently with accuracy, that the genealogy drawn up at Compiègne was faulty in that it made Ingeburg a descendant from Canute, the son of Swegn, whereas she was a descendant of his brother Eric.[31] Ingeburg by the hand of William also wrote to Celestine, declaring that her "happiness incited the envy of the enemy of the human race" and he had thrown "her to earth like a branch withered and dry." Her husband had left her although he found no fault with her except that fabricated by deceit.[32]

Again, in 1194 William wrote to Celestine saying that he, "whose heart was broken by the blows of sadness day and night," was appealing to the Apostolic See, where the successor of Peter "poured out the dew of his blessing on his parched body." "I exhort you, most clement Father," he continued, "to restore thy daughter in the full measure of your glory, and, by the mediation of justice, to put down him by whom I am afflicted so that she be reconciled, and the credit of the reconciliation be accorded to God and to the grace of your Paternity." [33] Emissaries also were sent to Celestine by King Canute.[34]

---

[29] Guillelmus Neubrigensis, *Historia Anglicana*, R.S., I, 370.
[30] J. Langebek (ed.), *Scriptores Rerum Danicarum* (Hafnia, 1772–1834), VI, 92.
[31] *Ibid.*   [32] *Ibid.*, 28.   [33] *Ibid.*
[34] *Gesta Innocentii Tercii*, in Migne, *P.L.*, CCXIV, col. L.

Impelled to activity by the frequency and earnest-
ness of the appeals, Celestine on May 13, 1195, wrote to
William, Archbishop of Rheims. He recounted the
previous devotion of the French kings to the pope and
the papacy's efforts in their behalf.[35] He declared that
marriage was a divine institution and that divorce, except where adultery was proved, was in contravention
to God's commands. He bemoaned the fact that the
queen, after being espoused with oaths and legitimately
married, had been subsequently repudiated. The pontiff
admonished the archbishop to order the French clergy
to prevent Philip from contracting another marriage.
This of course was tantamount to a revocation of the
declaration of nullity procured at Compiègne.

About the same time the pope wrote to Philip declaring that "having examined the document concerning
Ingeburg's genealogy, transmitted to us by the Archbishop of Lund and his suffragans, and having regard
for public reputation, we are exasperated and quash the
sentence of nullity pronounced against the order of the
law by the wicked counsels of our brothers." Philip was
enjoined to reinstate Ingeburg "for God and the salvation of his soul" and was exhorted to treat her with
marital affection. The pontiff explained that surely even
Philip must know that the Apostolic See could "not pass
this by with closed eyes saving our consciences and without peril to your soul." [36]

The pope finally dispatched Centius to France in the
spring of 1196, and a council of archbishops, bishops,
and abbots was held in which "they deliberated concern-

---

[35] Langebek, *Scriptores Rerum Danicarum*, VI, 82–84.
[36] *Ibid.*, 85–86.

ing the reforming of the marriage between King Philip
and his wife, Ingeburg. But because they were mute
dogs, not daring to bark, and fearing ever for their
skins, they brought nothing to conclusion." [37]

In June, 1196, Philip married Agnes of Meran in defiance of the pope's prohibition.[38] Again protests came
to Celestine. William the Abbot wrote complaining that
Philip's perfidy was well known and declaring that since
the Apostolic See was pre-eminent in dignity, it "ought
to provide more diligently in giving judgment, so that
in the carrying on of business and in the treatment of
matters, it on no account leave the law of justice, in the
way of truth and equity, for the sake of love or hate." [39]
He also wrote to the cardinals at Rome extolling the
Papal Curia as the haven of the oppressed but expressing dissatisfaction with the manner in which Ingeburg's
cause had been handled.[40]

Ingeburg, too, had reason to complain at the turn
events had taken. She wrote that three years had elapsed
since the king had married her and "since he had extended to her the required marital duties." She went on
to say that "by diabolical instigation and the persuasion
of the Prince of Evil he married Agnes of Meran and
retained her as his wife and ordered me confined in a
castle where I spend the time thus banished, where I
neither dare, nor can, raise my eyes to heaven. He al-
leges nothing except kinship, and no charge of any abuse
for which I ought to be separated from him, but he

---

[37] Rigordus, *Gesta Philippi Augusti, Soc. hist. Fr.*, II, 125.
[38] *Ibid.; Gesta Innocentii Tercii*, in Migne, *P.L.*, CCXIV, col. L;
Roger de Hoveden, *Chronica, R.S.*, III, 307.
[39] Langebek, *Scriptores Rerum Danicarum*, VI, 27.
[40] *Ibid.*, 28.

makes a decree of a wish, a law of willfulness, and a passion of voluptuousness." "I grieve therefore," continued her pitiful appeal, "and I eat bread with sadness and am compelled to mix my drink continually with tears, and I do this not for myself, but because of the king who gave an example of malignity to the orthodox faith and to the Christians and to all his realm." She declared that unless aid soon were extended to her she would die.[41]

The queen's appeals remained unanswered. It was not until the accession of the vigorous Innocent III that her hopes again were raised. Celestine, although doubtless sympathizing with Ingeburg and deprecating Philip's actions, was too timid to undertake the task of coercing the recalcitrant king into compliance with the papal orders. His successor was his antithesis—he was young, vigorous, courageous, imbued with the loftiest conception of the duties of his office, and eager to assert his authority over princes.

Soon after Innocent's accession an embassy was sent to him by King Canute pleading for papal intervention in behalf of Ingeburg.[42] The pontiff responded by ordering the Bishop of Paris to endeavor to persuade Philip to take back his legitimate wife and dismiss Agnes of Meran. He also was directed to point out to the king that any children he begot from Agnes would be illegitimate, and hence, if his only son, Louis, were to die, his kingdom would devolve upon strangers.[43]

The pope soon after wrote to Philip himself. He spoke of his great love for France, where he had studied

[41] *Ibid.*, 85.   [42] *R.H.F.*, XVII, 596.
[43] Migne, *P.L.*, CCXIV, 3–5.

in his youth, and of the pleasant memories he had there-
from. He recalled to the king his predecessors' obedience and devotion to the Holy See. He attributed the
misfortunes which were besetting Philip to God's displeasure at the repudiation of his legitimate wife and
his subsequent illegal marriage. He reviewed his abortive effort to reconcile the king to his wife through the
mediation of the Bishop of Paris and exhorted Philip
to comply with his direct order "in remission of his
sins." In the event that the king did not obey the papal
orders the pontiff declared that he would not hesitate
"to do what we owe to our duty." [44] Thus, while the
letter was conciliatory and persuasive rather than mandatory, its close clearly hinted at ecclesiastical censure,
which would be utilized to coerce the recalcitrant king if
he did not prove amenable to milder measures. Another
letter soon followed in which the king was censured for
his failure to obey the Bishop of Paris. The pope also
took occasion to bemoan the strained relations between
France and England, which he attributed to Philip's
sin. [45]

About the same time his first letter to Philip was
written, the pope wrote to Peter of Capua, his legate,
ordering him to insist that Philip take back Ingeburg
as his wife and treat her with conjugal affection. He
was to be given one month in which to comply, and in
the event that he persisted in his obduracy, an interdict
was to be laid on his kingdom. [46]

The legate was delayed either because of the press
of his duties to preach the Fourth Crusade or by illness;
his arrival in France therefore did not occur before

[44] *Ibid.*, 148–50.   [45] *Ibid.*, 148–50, 321–22.   [46] *Ibid.*, 320–21.

Easter, 1199. Other affairs, principally the endeavor to establish a truce between Philip and King Richard of England, occupied the legate, so that it was not until December of 1199 that a council was convoked at Dijon to deal with the marital question.[47] A stringent interdict was decided upon, which was formally promulgated at Vienne.[48] Only baptism of infants and the confession and absolution of the dying were allowed. Mass was to be said to consecrate the bread for the sick, and priests were allowed to enter the churches to keep the lamps and candles burning. Preaching was permitted on Sundays outside the churches, and confessions were heard on the church porches. Burial in consecrated ground was strictly forbidden as was the "churching" of women. Even on Easter there was to be no communion save for the sick.[49] Shortly after the promulgation of the interdict the pope exempted from its provisions those taking the cross for the projected crusade.[50]

The pope in a letter of October, 1199, had ordered the French clergy to obey the sentence when it was proclaimed. He declared that he had applied "the iron to wounds" which were not "sensible of the medicine of soothing applications." [51] After the interdict was formally imposed, Innocent confirmed it and threatened the clergy with deprivation if they transgressed its provisions.[52]

---

[47] *Gesta Innocentii Tercii*, in Migne, *P.L.*, CCXIV, col. LI; Radulphus de Diceto, *Ymagines Historiarum*, R.S., II, 168; Guillelmus Armoricus, *Gesta Philippi Augusti*, Soc. hist. Fr., II, 205.

[48] *Gesta Innocentii Tercii*, in Migne, *P.L.*, CCXIV, col. LI.

[49] E. Martène (ed.), *Thesaurus novus Anecdotorum* (Paris, 1717), IV, 147.

[50] Roger de Hoveden, *Chronica*, R.S., IV, 113.

[51] Migne, *P.L.*, CCXIV, 745–47.   [52] *Ibid.*, 747–48.

Philip tried to coerce and intimidate the clergy into disregard of the interdict with but partial success.[53] He also sent emissaries to the pope to secure relaxation of the sentence, but the pope could not be induced to modify the decree "by entreaty, prayer, bribe, threats, or promises." [54] Finally, Octavian was dispatched as legate with power to raise the interdict on certain conditions. Philip was to restore Ingeburg as his wife and queen and treat her with the proper conjugal affection. He also was to make adequate restitution to those whom he had persecuted because of their observance of the papal decree, and Agnes was to be banished from the kingdom. The legate also was directed to treat with Philip to establish peace between him and King John of England so as to prepare for the pope's projected crusade.[55]

The legate arrived in France in September, 1200.[56] He was received by the clergy and people with great joy and was treated with honor. The king, as soon as he was informed of the arrival of the papal representative, hastened to meet him and proved so humble and compliant that it was thought miraculous. The king in tears promised publicly to extend adequate compensation to those who had incurred damage by his efforts to force them to flout the interdict. He swore to have no intercourse with Agnes and promised not to meet her until his case was terminated. Ingeburg was then publicly received as his wife and queen at St. Leodegarius, where French queens were accustomed to celebrate the principal

[53] Radulfus de Coggeshall, *Chronicon Anglicanum*, R.S., 112.
[54] *Ibid.*
[55] *Gesta Innocentii Tercii*, in Migne, *P.L.*, CCXIV, col. LIV; *Migne, P.L.*, CCXIV, 887–91.
[56] Roger de Hoveden, *Chronica*, R.S., IV, 137.

feasts. She was ill and asked to have the ceremony there
rather than at Paris. The king, after public reconciliation with her, caused one of his knights to swear for him
that he would not subsequently separate from her without judgment of the Church. The legate then ordained
that an assembly be held six months later at Soissons to
deliberate concerning a declaration of nullity.[57]

Innocent was not quite satisfied with the actions of
his legate. In a letter of October, 1200, he chided Octavian because he had not insisted on the banishment of
Agnes from the kingdom, since her continued presence
in France might give the impression that the Holy See
was condoning bigamy. Then, too, as Innocent learned
from a letter of Ingeburg, the unfortunate queen was
really in captivity again and was not treated with respect. She had but two Danish chaplains in her entourage, and with these she was compelled to converse in
French in the presence of Philip's retainers. Philip had
also forbidden his subjects to say prayers for the queen.[58]

Her restoration had been merely a verbal one; she
was now more heavily laden than before. Innocent
seemed inclined to blame the legate for these conditions,
censuring him for not insisting on Paris as the scene of
the reconciliation. He also seemed to think that the
legate had been too prompt in raising the interdict. He
therefore ordered Octavian to take measures to insure
better treatment for the queen and bade him remember
that he had indicated to him verbally how the case
would redound to the prestige of the Holy See if
handled correctly and, conversely, how much scandal
would be entailed if the case were not brought to a

[57] Migne, *P.L.*, CCXIV, 887–90.   [58] *Ibid.*, 891–95.

proper and equitable termination. The legate was exhorted to take the case more to heart and to be actuated
more by consideration for his own salvation than by a
desire to please the king.[59]

Philip evidently had practiced the most palpable
circumlocution. Innocent, however, was not free to re-
establish the interdict since, as his legate had reported,
there was danger that parts of France would break with
Rome on the question.[60] Then, too, heresy was rife in
southern France, and anything which might lead to
augmentation of discontent with the Church had to be
allayed. The pontiff's desire to secure Philip's support
for Otto of Brunswick against Philip of Swabia also precluded the exercise of rigor at this juncture.[61]

The pope confined himself to the more immediate
interest of the impending Council of Soissons. On October 19, 1200, he wrote to King Canute. After expressing his esteem for the Danish sovereign, the pontiff recounted his efforts in Ingeburg's behalf. Philip had
charged that Ingeburg was related to him within the
prohibited degrees, and the matter would have to be
tried in accordance with the canons. He asked Canute to
transmit suitable replies to the allegations of Philip, as
well as advocates and witnesses and everything else that
might aid Ingeburg's defense. He was requested to endeavor to prove false the charges of impotence and affinity which Philip had brought forward to justify the
separation. He was admonished not to neglect to take
these measures lest his sister's cause be jeopardized.[62]

---

[59] *Ibid.*   [60] *Ibid.*, 887.
[61] Davidsohn, *Philip II und Ingeburg*, 151.
[62] Migne, *P.L.*, CCXIV, 883-84.

On the following day a letter was dispatched to Ingeburg. The pope summarized his past efforts in the case,
emphasizing the recent interdict, which he likened to
the oil and wine which the Good Samaritan used to
soothe the wounds of the man by the wayside. He re-
assured her that she could not be dismissed again without impartial judgment.[63]

A short time later the pontiff wrote to Philip. He expressed the ardent wish that Philip "would learn, or
be shown by his followers, how much honor, glory,
praise, and fame would redound to him were he zealous
in the execution of the papal orders." To be sure, the
king was to be commended because he had "honored the
Apostolic See in the observance of catholic discipline,
humbly obeying orders of the Vicar of Jesus Christ who
bestowed on him the temporal life and would bestow on
him the future life" when he acceded to the demands
of Octavian. The legate's orders had not been an act
of violence, "but justice, or rather, medicine, which
when it had fully worked, was going to make him more
obedient than ever." He exhorted Philip to take back
Ingeburg since he could not espouse a more "honest or
more noble woman, who is not only reputed good, but
holy." If Philip still desired to be separated from his
wife, the pope promised to have judgment pronounced
canonically, with all precautions to insure against mis-
handling, which would damage both the pope's and the
king's reputations.[64]

In March, 1201, the council assembled at Soissons,
under the presidency of Octavian. Both Philip and Inge-

[63] *Ibid.*, 881–82.   [64] *Ibid.*, 896–97.

burg were in attendance.[65] Canute had sent "bishops
and other honest and discreet men" to testify for his
sister. These envoys asked Philip to accord them freedom to "respond, allege, and leave the land," which
privileges were forthwith granted to them. Philip then
formally asked for nullification of the marriage on the
grounds of affinity. The Danish emissaries based their
defense on the charge that Philip was perjured and
guilty of bad faith since, after contracting by oath to
marry Ingeburg, he had repudiated her and broken his
oath. The Danes then objected to the legate on the
grounds that he was a relative of Philip and appealed to
the pope. A new legate, Cardinal John of St. Paul's,
joined the assembly at about this time and shared the
presidency with Octavian.[66]

Despite the concession of an additional judge the
Danes withdrew, leaving Ingeburg defenseless, for an
annalist of the time says, "when there was no one in
the whole multitude who would plead for her because
of fear of the king, an unknown poor clerk, arising from
their midst, with permission of the king and cardinals,
argued the case of the queen most eloquently so that he
was admired by the king himself and by the cardinals
and bishops." The statement by the same annalist that
the queen "had no advocate except God when the council opened" is erroneous.[67] The deliberations continued
fifteen days, when, "after varied and many disputes of

---

[65] *Annales Aquicinctensis*, in *R.H.F.*, XVIII, 552; Rigordus, *Gesta
Philippi Augusti*, Soc. hist. Fr., II, 149.

[66] Roger de Hoveden, *Chronica*, R.S., IV, 148.

[67] J. Harduin (ed.), *Conciliorum Collectio regia maxima* (Paris,
1715), VI, Pt. II, col. 1966.

those learned in the law, the king, affected by ennui at the long delay" left the council in the company of Ingeburg, telling the ecclesiastics by messenger "that he took his wife with him, and he did not wish to be separated from her. Having heard this, the council was dissolved, to the amazement of the cardinals and bishops who had come together to pronounce a divorce . . . and so King Philip escaped the hand of the Romans by this act." [68] Philip, by his disavowal of the desire for a declaration of nullity, had obviated the possibility of further action at the time. His reconciliation was merely simulated, for Ingeburg was immediately reincarcerated.[69]

In November, 1201, Philip's children by Agnes of Meran were declared legitimate by the pope with the understanding that this action in no way impugned the validity of the king's marriage to Ingeburg.[70]

The king's representatives continued to agitate at the papal court for the dissolution of the marriage, and finally their transmission of Philip's complaint that he had been more severely treated by the pope than other princes had been in similar cases provoked Innocent to reply on July 5, 1202. The pontiff expressed grief that Philip complained "concerning that in which we both merited and expected deeds of gratitude." In regard to the assertion that Philip had been harshly treated, the pope declared that while it was true that Frederick I of Germany had obtained a separation from a woman reputed to be his wife, this was granted by a legate of the Holy See and no criticisms had been made of the deci-

---

[68] Rigordus, *Gesta Philippi Augusti*, Soc. hist. Fr., II, 149.

[69] Roger de Hoveden, *Chronica*, R.S., IV, 148.

[70] Migne, *P.L.*, CCXIV, 1191–94; L. Deslisle (ed.), *Catalogue des actes de Philippe Auguste* (Paris, 1856), Nos. 698, 699, 704, 711.

sion. In the case of Louis VII of France the matter had
not been brought to the attention of the pope since
neither of the parties appealed from the decision of the
local clergy. "But whether or not the Apostolic See is
able to dissemble the strivings of oppressors of sick
women, the king himself may know or may be better
guided by his counselors," continued the pope. Philip
was actuated "not by reason but by sensuality, since he
called equity severity, and justice violence." The pope
insisted on his right to revoke a sentence of nullity illegally pronounced, citing as a precedent the case of
Lothair II. The king was informed that two legates
were to be dispatched to Étampes, where the queen was
held in custody, in order to receive her depositions in
regard to the allegations of affinity.[71]

If Ingeburg desired, she was to have advocates and
witnesses, and lest Canute excuse himself from sending
witnesses, the pope declared that he had sent men to
Denmark to receive depositions in the queen's behalf.
If Philip preferred and Ingeburg consented, the pope
declared that he would allow the legates to choose men
from France to settle the case provided no abuse arose
which would necessitate the revocation of their sentence.[72] Innocent obviously was willing to allow almost
any kind of procedure to settle the matter provided the
queen was satisfied, but he made it clear that no matter
how much latitude was accorded as to ways and means
Ingeburg was to have a fair hearing.

In May, 1203, Ingeburg wrote a letter to the pope
which even yet moves us to pity. She called herself the
least of Innocent's children, a queen in name only. The

---

[71] Migne, *P.L.*, CCXIV, 1015–17.   [72] *Ibid.*

pope, she avowed, had helped her bear her cross; he was "a mountain placed on the top of mountains towards which her eyes were raised, a supporter of the oppressed, a refuge of the miserable." She pleaded for liberation from those that hated her, declaring that her husband, after imprisoning her, had not ceased to vex her by the contumely and opprobrium cast on her by his followers. She was not allowed to see anyone, nor was she even allowed to have divine services for the refreshment of her soul, and only rarely did she hear mass. No Dane could approach her, not even her physician although she was ill. She was forced to listen to the obscene talk of Philip's retainers. Finally, with a feminine touch she complained that she did not have clothes befitting her station. She declared that she wanted either relief or death, for her present condition was unendurable.[73]

In a letter of July 5, 1205, addressed to Ingeburg, the pope explained that he had made little progress in reconciling her husband with her. Philip was now alleging that sorcery had prevented him from entering into full marital relations with his wife and proffered this as grounds for nullity of the union. Innocent assured the queen that he had refused to annul the marriage on the strength of this latest allegation of the king, but "he could not change the will of God or hurry it." He went on to say that he was sending his chaplain to her to extend solace, and she could communicate through him with the Holy See.[74]

The pope wrote another letter to Philip on April 2, 1207. He declared that "the duty of our pastoral office,

[73] Ibid., CCXV, 86–88.   [74] Ibid., 680.

by which we are debtor both to the wise and the foolish, moves us to impell your regal magnificence by warnings concerning those things which are just and honest. Although we had often urged your gentleness that you recall your queen and wife in full favor by God's grace, you gave attention to but part of the Apostle's warnings." The recalcitrant king had not as yet shown conjugal favor to his wife, so that even among men in his confidence he was hard pressed to find excuses for his derelictions. The Gospel did not teach that women were to be degraded and defrauded. The pontiff admonished Philip to attempt again to establish full marital relations with his wife and went on to say that "if indeed you have God who does not err as a witness of your conscience that you cannot treat her with this kind of favor, then be overcome with shame so that you do not allow this illustrious woman, niece of a king, sister of a king, and wife of a king, to be held as a captive." He warned the king that if he continued to deal fraudulently with her both the world and God would judge him, "one of which he could placate by penitence, the other he could hardly restrain if He rose against him." [75]

In November or December of 1207 Innocent informed Philip that he would sanction his projected attempt to have carnal intercourse with Ingeburg. He assured him that the attempt would in no wise endanger his prospects for annulment no matter what the outcome might be. He advised Philip to pray and offer alms so that divine favor might be invoked in his aid and the impediment of sorcery which prevented the carnal intercourse might be overcome.[76]

[75] *Ibid.*, 1135–36.   [76] *Ibid.*, 1266.

In May, 1208, the pope ordered his legate, Gualo, to investigate the alleged enchantment which Philip asserted had hindered him from coition with his wife. The legate was first to liberate the queen from imprisonment and was then to proceed to the examination. If both parties agreed, the pope authorized the legate to pronounce a definitive sentence; otherwise he was to submit the results of his examination to the pope after assigning to the parties a date on which to receive sentence.[77] The plans for settling the case proved abortive, for Innocent was forced to temporize since he needed Philip's support against John of England.

Philip continued to press the pope for a declaration of nullity. On December 7, 1208, he wrote asking that Gualo be given the power to dissolve the marriage because of affinity, sorcery, or Ingeburg's desire to embrace the religious life, "or by any other reasonable means whereby marriage was wont to be dissolved in your time and in the days of your predecessors." The king urged the pope to grant the annulment, which he could easily do if he so willed. Philip obviously was endeavouring to secure a separation by papal dictum without the formality of a trial. Innocent was still willing to have the case heard, but he constantly had insisted that there could be no declaration of nullity without an impartial trial in which Ingeburg would be afforded ample opportunity to defend herself. He therefore replied to the king's request by advising him to seek more prudent counsel.[78]

Philip was becoming impatient. In January, 1209, he wrote to Gualo, complaining of the reception of a

[77] *Ibid.*, 1403.   [78] *Ibid.*, 1493.

legate he had dispatched to the pope. He inveighed against the procrastination of the Holy See and declared that "because it seems that the pope does not wish to free us or be helpful to us, we order that you do not tarry in these regions unless you have the case for disposal." [79] The king had another card to play. Through his emissary he asked that he be allowed to marry another woman since Ingeburg voluntarily had turned to the religious life and since, as he had sworn, he had not been able to enjoy copulation with her.

The pontiff admitted in his reply that scripture and papal enactments justified such separation since "where the Spirit of God is, there is liberty"; and if the marriage had not been consummated, there would be no impediments for the other to remarry in the event that one party decided to embrace the celibate life, since without consummation no marriage had really taken place. Marriage consummated by sexual intercourse rendered a man and his wife one body, and this union was indissoluble "just as the union of truth and human nature is the dwelling within our body of truth, and truth cannot be separated from the body." On the other hand, marriage without corporeal consummation was analogous to the bond of charity between God and a just soul. He was adhered to God as of one spirit with Him, but this union was often sundered; likewise, a marriage wherein only agreement of the souls of the contracting parties was present was capable of dissolution. The weak point in Philip's case was his allegation of nonintercourse with Ingeburg since she had sworn that he had carnally known her. If she subsequently

[79] Deslisle, *Catalogue des actes de Philippe Auguste,* 515.

denied that the marriage had been consummated, the pope declared that he believed that her statement was made under duress. The pope elucidated that in case of denial of intercourse by one party to a marriage the burden of substantiating the allegation rested on the party that denied it, and Gregory VII in a similar case had demanded seven-handed compurgation to prove such a contention. The pope also expressed the belief that Ingeburg's avowed desire to enter a convent was in response to pressure put upon her by Philip. The king was informed, in the close of the letter, that Gualo was authorized to hear the case on any of the three grounds, that is, affinity, sorcery, or conversion to the religious life.[80]

Ingeburg's mistreatment continued unabated. On May 7, 1210, Innocent wrote to comfort her in her afflictions. "God was trying her courage," declared the pope, perhaps to prepare her to bear still greater trials. The queen was admonished to be patient since patience and fortitude in the face of adversity would do most to influence God to move the heart of the king to reinstate her in his affections.[81]

On June 9, 1212, the pope dispatched a letter to his legate, Guarinus, who was then in Gaul. He complained that Philip, "led by perverters of truth and enemies of justice," had been convinced that he could legitimately swear that he had not carnally known his queen "because an admixture of sexes had not taken place" since "*commistio tamen seminum in vase miliebri non extitit subsecuta.*" The legate was ordered to exhort Philip "to avert his hearing from insanities of this kind" and was

[80] Migne, *P.L.*, CCXV, 1494–98.   [81] *Ibid.*, CCXVI, 258–59.

bidden to "advance in goodness him who we believe has a sincere soul." [82]

On the same day Innocent wrote to Philip, who again had sent agents to the Holy See to secure annulment of the marriage. The pope stated that "in those things which they asked from us . . . we would strive most gladly with God, under the admonition of divine judgment, to free you from the chain from which you so earnestly wish to be loosed." Even if Ingeburg's allegations concerning the consummation of the marriage were false, the Gospels, the Fathers, and the Saints conjoined in denying him the power to dissolve the marriage without the sanction of a general council. In the event that the pontiff should have the temerity to pronounce a sentence of nullity, there would be both "divine offense and worldly odium" for him and "peril of our office and order would be imminent." The king was admonished to disregard the promptings of evil counselors, who did not dare speak the truth because of fear, and was urged to heed instead the orders of the pope who was responsible for the royal soul on the dread day of judgment. Philip once more was commanded to treat Ingeburg according to the marriage law and was not to make matters more difficult for the pope.[83]

Philip made no further attempt to secure a divorce. In April, 1213, when he was meeting his vassals at Soissons to receive their pledges to aid him on his projected invasion of England, he publicly received Ingeburg as his wife.[84] This action was connected with the invasion

---

[82] *Ibid.*, 618.   [83] *Ibid.*, 617–18.

[84] Guillelmus Armoricus, *Gesta Philippi Augusti*, Soc. hist. Fr., II, 247; Robertus Altissiodoris, *Chronica*, in *R.H.F.*, XVIII, 281.

of England since Philip, who was to undertake the expedition under the auspices of the Holy See, naturally would wish to remove the only current point of dispute between him and the pontiff.[85]

Despite the frustration of his designs on England by King John's submission and by the consequent alteration of papal policy, Philip adequately provided for Ingeburg for the rest of her days although he never had full conjugal relations with her. After her death in 1218, he established ecclesiastical endowments to the sum of six thousand livres to commemorate her love.[86]

Innocent's bitterest and most spectacular struggle to enforce the marital laws had fallen short of complete success. His intervention had been prompt and forceful, but neither cajolery nor coercion sufficed fully to attain his objectives. To be sure, the repudiation of Agnes had resulted from the interdict, but even this sentence, the most potent weapon in the garner of the Church, succeeded in coercing Philip into only partial submission to the papal mandate to restore Ingeburg as his wife and queen. Reluctance to alienate the king permanently because his support was desired for papal policies such as the crusade, the suppression of heresy, and the cause of Otto in Germany doubtless impelled the pope to condone Philip's recalcitrance to some degree.

The pope's sympathies were consistently with Ingeburg, but he evinced a desire to propitiate Philip by granting him every opportunity, consonant with the law, of securing a declaration of nullity. Never, however,

---

[85] Davidsohn, *Philip II und Ingeburg*, 251 ff.

[86] Guillelmus Armoricus, *Gesta Philippi Augusti*, Soc. hist. Fr., II, 247; Deslisle, *Catalogue des actes de Philippe Auguste*, No. 1218.

did he consent, even by implication, to any action that deprived Ingeburg of the right to a fair, impartial hearing of her case, nor did he cease to deprecate her mistreatment, which, however, he could not mitigate by entreaty or compulsion. Innocent did not sacrifice Ingeburg to political expediency; even when Philip's support was most ardently desired, the pontiff was adamant in his refusal to pronounce a decree which would have been the surest way of securing the king's allegiance. Political considerations, redounding to the good of the Church, however, were the dominant motives in inducing the pope to refrain from unremitting attempts to coerce Philip into complete compliance with the papal demands. The experiences of the interdict, which had been productive of schism and discord among the French clergy, would have been sufficient to deter him from a repetition of this action.

CHAPTER VII

INNOCENT'S ENFORCEMENT IN SPAIN AND BOHEMIA

INNOCENT'S endeavors to enforce the marriage laws in Spain were considerably more successful than in France. King Alfonso IX of Leon (1188–1230), towards the end of 1190, married his niece, Theresa, daughter of King Sancho of Portugal, as a means of consolidating the peace between these two realms. A short time after his accession to the papal throne, Celestine III ordered the dissolution of the marriage.[1] A council was thereupon held at Salamanca under the presidency of the resident legate of the Holy See, and after careful examination the marriage was nullified.[2] Alfonso obdurately refused to separate from his wife. His kingdom thereupon was placed under an interdict, and both he and his queen were excommunicated.[3] Despite these measures he continued to live with his wife for five years.[4]

About 1195 Alfonso became embroiled in a war with the King of Castile (Alfonso VIII, 1158–1214), which

---

[1] Roger de Hoveden, *Chronica*, R.S., III, 90.

[2] J. Aguirre (ed.), *Collectio Maxima Conciliorum Omnium Hispaniae* (Ibarra, 1785), V, 104.

[3] Roger de Hoveden, *Chronica*, R.S., III, 90; Migne, *P.L.*, CCXIV, 51.

[4] Roger de Hoveden, *Chronica*, R.S., III, 90.

resulted in much devastation.[5] Roger de Hoveden declared that the King of Castile then compelled Alfonso of Leon to divorce Theresa in order that he might marry his daughter, Berengaria, a relative in the second degree of consanguinity.[6] While it is not clearly established that the King of Castile compelled him to separate from Theresa, it is certain that he did dismiss her about this time, and she returned to Portugal at the end of 1195. The excommunications and interdict were thereupon lifted.[7]

Early in 1197, in order to insure peace between the warring realms, Alfonso married Berengaria,[8] not with the pope's permission as Roger de Hoveden narrated,[9] but despite the prohibition of the resident legate who excommunicated the king and several Spanish bishops who condoned the illicit marriage.[10]

This was the situation when Innocent ascended the pontifical throne. On April 16, 1198, the pope wrote to Rainerius, the legate whom he was sending to Spain. The pontiff first regaled the legate with a homily on the frequency with which the Lord chose his servants from among the humble, even deigning to elevate him to the pontifical throne, "raising him up from dung and lifting him from the dust." He declared that the task of re-establishing peace in Spain as well as another of

---

[5] Rodericus Toletanus, *De Rebus Hispaniae* (ed. Bel), VII, c. 24; Luca Tudensis, *Chronicon Mundi* (ed. Schottus), III; IV, 109.

[6] Roger de Hoveden, *Chronica, R.S.,* III, 90.

[7] H. Florez (ed.), *España sagrada. Theatro geogr.-historico de la iglesia de España* (Madrid, 1754–1866), XXXV, 261.

[8] Rodericus Toletanus, *De Rebus Hispaniae,* VII, c. 24.

[9] Roger de Hoveden, *Chronica, R.S.,* III, 90.

[10] Florez, *España sagrada,* XXXV, 263–64.

greater moment had been committed to him. The King
of Leon had presumed to marry his niece, Berengaria,
"trusting the strength of his arm and believing through
it to banish the imminent chastisement." The legate was
ordered to revoke "that wicked contract, abominable in
the sight of God and detestable in the judgment of the
faithful." [11]

The legate was directed to dissolve "all bonds of im-
piety which were concluded between them under this
species of incest, all delay and excuse being abrogated."
In the event that the kings of Leon and Castile were
contumacious, the pope directed that they be excommunicated and their lands placed under an interdict.
Rainerius was also instructed to coerce the King of
Aragon by the threat of interdict so that he would cease
his aggressions against the ruler of Leon. [12]

Immediately after his arrival in Leon, Rainerius cited
the king to appear before him on an appointed day. Alfonso refused to take cognizance of the citation and was
at once excommunicated, and an interdict was placed on
his kingdom. The King of Castile avoided the imminent penalty by expressing his willingness to take back
his daughter if Alfonso of Leon would agree to an annulment of the marriage. [13]

Innocent apparently anticipated the immediate compliance of the King of Leon as a result of these coercive
measures, for on April 21, 1198, he wrote to Rainerius
directing him to suspend the excommunication and to
mitigate the severity of the interdict just as soon as he

[11] Migne, *P.L.*, CCXIV, 79, 80.   [12] *Ibid.*

[13] *Gesta Innocentii Tercii*, in Migne, *P.L.*, CCXIV, col. LVIII.

received adequate guarantee that the incestuous union would be dissolved.[14]

A new complication was soon introduced. The Bishop of Orvieto, because he had "obeyed and caused to be observed the interdict promulgated by the authority of the Holy See," had been "compelled to undergo exile which was neither just nor honest." The king's absolution therefore was made contingent upon his agreement to accord the exiled bishop the liberty to resume the administration of his see. Adequate restitution was to be made for damages the prelate had incurred because of his devotion to papal policies.[15]

During Celestine's last days emissaries apparently had been dispatched to Rome to secure a dispensation permitting the uncanonical marriage to continue. They had remained in Rome after Celestine's death but had great difficulty in securing an audience with Innocent because of the aversion the new pontiff manifested to the object of their mission.[16]

On May 25, 1199, the pope sent a letter to the Archbishop of Compostello and other Spanish prelates in which he discussed the efforts of the king's representatives to secure a dispensation. The pontiff declared that "indeed, the tumults and scandals in our days surprise the whole world, today more manifested in fact than we find written in a book. . . . But it is necessary that scandal come, which, indeed, is not alone inevitable, but useful, since wherever evil loses, good gains, and the gold is proven in the furnace." The pope recalled to

---

[14] Migne, *P.L.*, CCXIV, 81.   [15] *Ibid.*, 115.

[16] Florez, *España sagrada*, XXXV, 264.

the minds of the Spanish clergy that the Lord had struck
with death princes of the East who, with the connivance of the clergy, had contracted incestuous marriages; but in the West no such punishment had as yet
been visited upon "the workers of iniquity who try His
patience."

A recapitulation of the history of the king's marital
affairs then followed, after which the pope discussed the
plea of the embassy to Rome. The royal representatives
had asked for a dispensation, or at least an amelioration
of the condition of the Spanish Church which was sorely
tried by the interdict. It was charged that the interdict
fomented heresy because of the inability of the people
to be inculcated with true doctrine after the closing of
the churches. It was also alleged that the interdict induced relaxation of the efforts to expel the Saracens.

Innocent expressed grave doubts as to the accuracy of
these depositions, but in order "to try their spirits to see
if they are of God," he authorized a considerable allevia-
tion of the severity of the interdict. Divine services and
the bestowal of the sacraments were permitted, but
burial in consecrated ground was still forbidden except
to the clergy. In order that these concessions might not
seem equivalent to a complete cessation of the interdict,
the pope directed that divine services be prohibited
wherever the king and queen and their chief abettors
chanced to be, thus transforming the interdict from the
general to the ambulatory form.[17] The statement of
Roger de Hoveden that Alfonso's emissaries had offered two thousand marks of silver and two hundred
knights for one year's service in the Holy Land seems

[17] Migne, *P.L.*, CCXIV, 610–15.

unfounded since there is no reference to this proposal in Innocent's letter.[18]

Alfonso remained obdurate.[19] In 1202 he presided over a Cortes at Benaventum, where he was accompanied by the queen, and the laws issued there were promulgated in the names of both himself and Berengaria.[20]

Innocent next turned his attention to the King of Castile who seemed to be more amenable to correction. In a letter dated June 5, 1203, the pope declared that "prudence without peril was sterile, but power without wisdom was odious." He ordered the king to do what he could to have the incestuous marriage between his daughter and the King of Leon revoked in order to avoid ecclesiastical censures, but nothing came of this effort.[21]

While Alfonso of Leon was impervious to ecclesiastical censures, his wife proved more pliable. In the spring of 1204 she separated from her spouse and petitioned the pope for absolution.[22] Innocent hastened to comply with her request. In a letter dated May 22, 1204, addressed to the Archbishop of Toledo and some of his suffragans, he declared that the precepts of Christ, "who did not wish the death of the sinner, but that he, converted, might live," impelled him "to act mercifully with those who wish humbly to return to the breast of

---

[18] Roger de Hoveden, *Chronica, R.S.,* IV, 79.

[19] Guillelmus Zamorae, *Vita Alfonsi IX,* in *Boletin de la Real Academia de la Historia,* XIII, 291.

[20] *Cortes de los antiguos reinos de Leon y de Castilla* (Madrid, 1861), I, 43.

[21] Migne, *P.L.,* CCXV, 82–83.

[22] Florez, *España sagrada,* XXXV, 264.

Mother Church." Although Berengaria "had gravely offended her Creator when she presumed to cleave to the illustrious King of Leon in incest, and because of this she deserved to be bound by the chain of excommunication," she had evinced adequate contrition by her withdrawal from marital relations with her husband and by her promise to do penance. The pope therefore ordered that her petition for absolution be granted, and the bishops were instructed to pronounce it publicly after receiving suitable pledges for her future good conduct.[23]

On June 19, 1204, the pope ordered the Archbishop of Compostello and other prelates to absolve Alfonso and raise the partial interdict which was still in force. His principal supporters who had been stricken by the same sentence were also absolved as were those who had incurred excommunication by refusing to shun the king. The only condition placed on the absolution was that Alfonso was required to swear never to return to Berengaria nor to receive her should she wish to return to him.[24] The oath was taken, and the absolutions were proclaimed together with a cessation of the interdict.[25]

One difficulty remained in connection with certain towns which Alfonso had assigned as a marriage gift to Berengaria and which the King of Castile was loath to have returned. Innocent, in a letter dated June 20, 1204, ordered immediate restitution of the towns; since the marriage had been invalid, the marriage gift had also been *ipso facto* voided. In the event that Berengaria alleged facts that would extenuate failure to hand

---

[23] Migne, *P.L.*, CCXV, 345–46.   [24] *Ibid.*, 376.   [25] *Ibid.*

back the towns, the matter was to be settled by arbiters chosen by each side or submitted to the pope for decision. Failure to comply with either of the alternatives suggested by the pope was to be punishable by excommunication of the parties.[26] The matter apparently was amicably adjusted, for nothing further was written by the pontiff on the subject.

Some time after the settlement of the marital case involving the kings of Leon and Castile, a curious litigation arose in Aragon. King Peter II of that country informed the pope that, impelled by pangs of conscience, he contemplated separation from his wife, Mary, on the grounds that she had a former husband from whom she was not legally separated. Queen Mary in rebuttal alleged that she had a former husband to whom she had been married while still a young girl, but since he was related to her within the forbidden degrees and was married to two other women from whom he had neglected to secure legitimate separation, she declared that her former marriage had been a *de facto* union with no legal sanction.

In January, 1213, Innocent, to whom the depositions of both parties had been submitted, informed Peter that Mary's contentions were substantially correct. Her first husband had been related to her within the fourth degree and had still been legally wedded to another wife at the time he contracted with Mary. The pontiff also allayed Peter's misgivings as to the possibility of his wife being related to him within the prohibited degrees by informing him that no taint was attached to his

[26] *Ibid.*, 374–75.

marriage. He ordered Peter to take back his wife and treat her with marital affection, which he thereupon did.[27]

Innocent's intervention in Spanish marital affairs was completely successful. It was the censure of the Church that induced Berengaria to separate from Alfonso and thus sunder their illicit union. The problem of compelling separation was made easier since Alfonso's marriage probably had been entered upon at the insistence of the King of Castile. The question was less complicated with political considerations than was the case of Philip Augustus. The pope did not need the support of Alfonso for his larger political projects as he did that of the French king. To be sure, Innocent did not attain his end with the immediate, humble compliance of the king as he doubtless desired, but by the weakening of Berengaria a long drawn-out struggle was avoided. The pope's desire to see the contest against the Saracens in Spain continue unabated probably actuated him in materially relaxing the interdict which, as was contended, vitiated the Christian strength. It must also be remembered that the infraction of the marital canons was a palpable one which was never questioned; the sending of the embassy to procure a dispensation was public acknowledgment that the law was violated, and this fact made Innocent's task considerably easier.

The King of Bohemia and Lesser Princes

The attempt of King Ottocar of Bohemia to divorce his wife also necessitated Innocent's intervention. In

[27] J. Dumont (ed.), *Corps universel diplomatique du droit des gens* (Amsterdam, 1726–1731), I, 146–47.

1199 the king sought separation from his queen on the grounds of relationship, although he had lived with her for twenty years and had begotten children by her.[28] A council, summoned by the Archbishop of Prague, pronounced the marriage annulled in accordance with the king's wishes.[29] The divorced ruler immediately married Constance, a daughter of King Andrew of Hungary.[30]

Adela, the repudiated queen, at once appealed to Innocent, alleging that she had been debarred from testimony at the council by the king's soldiers who refused her admittance. She declared that the alleged consanguinity was false and petitioned the pope to coerce Ottocar into restoring her.

On September 15, 1199, the pontiff, in accordance with her appeal, wrote to the Archbishop of Magdeburg. He ordered the metropolitan to summon the parties and witnesses from whom he was to take testimony. The depositions so obtained were to be transmitted to the pope for examination.[31] Nothing further was heard of this case until 1206, and the question naturally arises as to the reason for this lack of action.

Innocent desired Ottocar's support for Otto of Brunswick, head of the Welf party in Germany who had claimed the German throne after the death of Henry VI in 1197. There were great obstacles to the attainment of the papal objective. On September 8, 1198, Ottocar

---

[28] *Canonicorum Pragensium Continuatio Cosmae*, in *M.G.H., SS.*, IX, 169; Migne, *P.L.*, CCXIV, 737.

[29] Migne, *P.L.*, CCXIV, 737.

[30] *Canonicorum Pragensium Continuatio Cosmae*, in *M.G.H., SS.*, IX, 169; Migne, *P.L.*, CCXIV, 737.

[31] Migne, *P.L.*, CCXIV, 737.

had been recognized as king of Bohemia by Philip of Swabia, brother of the late Henry VI, who was also trying to secure the German crown.[32] In return for this recognition Ottocar fought on the side of Philip in October, 1198.[33] The alliance was still further strengthened by the coronation of Ottocar in 1199 at the Diet of Nuremburg, held under the auspices of Philip.[34]

By 1203 Ottocar was won over to Otto's party to whom he did homage.[35] In 1205, disastrously defeated by Philip,[36] he hastened to return to his former allegiance, giving seven thousand marks as guarantee of his good behavior.[37] As can be seen, his policy was vacillating, but it still held out hope of his definite alignment with the papal party in the German civil war. This is probably the explanation of the fact that the marital question was held in abeyance by the pope.

A letter dated April 26, 1206, addressed to the Archbishop of Salzburg, narrated the steps taken in the marriage case since the matter was first brought to the attention of the pope in 1199. The Archbishop of Magdeburg, in accordance with the papal order of 1199, had cited the king to appear for a hearing of his case, but he had maltreated the messengers bearing the summons and had refused to appear. Some time later the king

---

[32] J. F. Böhmer (ed.), *Regesta Imperii* (Stuttgart, 1870), V, 9.

[33] *Annales Colonienses Maximi*, in *M.G.H., SS.*, XVII, 807.

[34] Böhmer, *Regesta Imperii*, V, 10; Gerlacus, *Chronicon sive Annales Bohemiae*, in *M.G.H., SS.*, XVII, 710.

[35] *Canonicorum Pragensium Continuatio Cosmae*, in *M.G.H., SS.*, IX, 169.

[36] *Annales Colonienses Maximi*, in *M.G.H., SS.*, XVII, 819; *Canonicorum Pragensium Continuatio Cosmae*, in *M.G.H., SS.*, IX, 169; Arnoldus Lubecensis, *Chronica Slavorum*, in *M.G.H., SS.*, XXI, 216.

[37] *Canonicorum Pragensium Continuatio Cosmae*, in *M.G.H., SS.*, IX, 169; Arnoldus Lubecensis, *Chronica Slavorum*, in *M.G.H., SS.*, XXI, 216.

"was corrected by God, and great adversity having arisen against him," he returned to his wife. At least one of his great adversities was doubtless his defeat by Philip in 1205. Smitten by contrition, the king declared, "I deserve this by my merit because I dismissed my legitimate wife without cause and because of this injured my sons and daughters." Then, "having convoked the magnates of his realm and the representatives of his wife's brother, he swore and caused his followers to swear that he would expel the concubine and restore the wife." Despite these fair promises, and although in a personal letter to the pope he had avowed his intention of taking back his legitimate wife, he failed to do so. The Archbishop of Salzburg was then ordered to hold a new trial and transmit the evidence therein secured to the Holy See for decision.[38]

In 1207 Ottocar's alliance with Philip of Swabia was cemented by the betrothal of Philip's daughter, Gunegundis, to Wenceslaus, son of the Bohemian ruler. This girl previously had been betrothed to the Count Palatine, and he, enraged by the plan to marry her to Wenceslaus, assassinated Philip in June, 1208.[39]

The death of Philip of Swabia enabled Innocent to prosecute the marital case more vigorously, and on December 12, 1208, he wrote to the archbishops of Cologne and Magdeburg. The king had been excommunicated by the local prelates for contumacy in disregarding the citations, but he had appealed, objecting to the judges delegated to hear the case. Innocent ordered

[38] Migne, *P.L.*, CCXV, 872–73.
[39] *Canonicorum Pragensium Continuatio Cosmae*, in *M.G.H.*, *SS.*, IX, 169; Heinricus Heimburgensis, *Annales*, in *M.G.H.*, *SS.*, XVII, 713.

an inquiry to determine if the royal objections were justified.[40]

The case then was argued by procurators at Rome, as stated in a letter of April, 1210. The king's representatives charged that Adela consented to the separation but afterwards changed her mind and appealed, alleging that she had been defrauded. Efforts also were made to substantiate the contention that consanguinity voided the marriage. The King of Hungary, whose daughter was Ottocar's second wife, was quite truculent since he was not represented at the hearings in Rome.[41] Before the question could be settled Adela died in 1211, and the matter was allowed to lapse.[42]

Another complicated marital case with which Innocent had to deal arose in connection with a projected marriage of the Prince of Norway. In 1199 the pope was asked to decide the question on the basis of a number of contentions submitted to him. The prince had espoused a girl while she was still below the necessary age for betrothal. The engagement was not announced, and in the meantime the girl, apparently under duress, was engaged to the uncle of her prospective husband. The uncle died before marrying the girl, but his betrothal to her, if legal, precluded her marriage to his nephew, the Norwegian prince, since the impediment of "public honesty" had been engendered. The prince appealed for a papal decision, but the pontiff confessed his inability to give an immediate answer and referred the case to the local clergy for examination. He formulated

---

[40] Migne, *P.L.*, CCXV, 1499–1500.   [41] *Ibid.*, CCXVI, 238–42.
[42] B. Bretholz, *Geschichte Böhmens und Mährens bis 1306* (Munich, 1912), I, 64.

certain principles to be followed in arriving at a decision. If the nephew had been betrothed to the girl before the uncle, and both betrothals had been concluded
before the girl reached the age of seven, the nephew had
the prior claim, and her subsequent betrothal to his uncle
would not serve to prevent marriage. If, however, the
uncle's engagement had been concluded after the girl
had reached the proper age for betrothal, the nephew's
claim even though it antedated that of his uncle would
be void.[43] The case dragged on until April, 1203, when,
upon testimony that the girl had been eight years of
age when she contracted her engagement with the prince
prior to her commitment to his uncle, the pope granted
permission to the prince to marry her.[44]

Startling revelations soon disrupted what was ostensibly an amicable settlement of the case. The pope was
informed by formal depositions of witnesses that the
uncle had lived with the girl and habitually had slept
with her, although it was alleged that she had not attained the age of consent and no carnal intercourse had
taken place. After living illicitly with the girl for some
time, the uncle had left her and had gone into foreign
parts, but he subsequently returned and married her
shortly before his death. After his death the girl had
gone back to her parents. While all this had been going
on, the Prince of Norway had also married; and, after
his wife's death, he returned to his first love, whom he
probably married in accordance with the pope's permission of 1203.[45] The pope therefore revoked his earlier
permission for the marriage after investigation substan-

---

[43] Migne, *P.L.*, CCXIV, 791-92.   [44] *Ibid.*, CCXV, 49-50.
[45] *Ibid.*, 534-37.

tiated the contention that the uncle of the prince had been in full marital relations with her after she had reached the age of consent.

On September 3, 1211, Innocent wrote to the Archbishop of Torres ordering him to interfere in the marital relations contracted by the Judge of Cagliari with the daughter of the Count of Guyon. The pope declared that the contracting parties were related within the prohibited degrees, and he ordered examination of the case and separation of the parties if the facts alleged as to the relationship were corroborated.[46] In addition to these marital cases terminated by Innocent, there were several cases in which action was begun by him and completed by his successor.

[46] *Ibid.*, CCXVI, 465–66.

CHAPTER VIII

ENFORCEMENT FROM INNOCENT TO BONIFACE VIII

THE Count of Flanders, just before his death, commended Margaret, his wife's sister, to the care of Bochardus of Avesnes.[1] Bochardus, who had a considerable reputation as a scholar, was also to act as tutor of the girl.[2] There were many suitors for the hand of the maiden, but it seemed most likely that she would be given in marriage to the Count of Salisbury. Bochardus opposed all projects to bestow her on a foreign prince and in 1212 married her himself. It appears that the marriage was regularly performed, and no opposition was manifested to the union. The Countess of Flanders seems to have accorded tacit sanction to the nuptials.[3]

There were, however, serious impediments to the marriage. Bochardus, although he had been knighted by Richard the Lion Heart and had gained a great reputation as a soldier, once had taken orders, and this fact was known in Flanders at the time of the marriage. Then, too, the couple probably were related within the forbidden degrees.[4] When the relations between Margaret

---

[1] Migne, *P.L.*, CCXVI, 529.
[2] Jacobus de Guisia, *Annales Hanoniae*, in *M.G.H.*, *SS.*, XXX, Lib. XX.
[3] *Ibid.*; L. Kervyn de Lettenhove, *Histoire de Flandre* (Brussels, 1847–1855), II, App., 547.
[4] Migne, *P.L.*, CCXVI, 529, 530–31.

and her sister, the countess, became strained, probably because of disputed inheritance to certain lands, the countess complained to Innocent about the marriage.[5] In her accusation the countess alleged that Bochardus abducted the girl and conveyed her into foreign parts where he cohabited with her. It was also charged that Bochardus had been a canon of the cathedral of Laon prior to his coming to Flanders and that he was related to Margaret within the prohibited degrees.[6]

In response to the complaint Innocent ordered the Bishop of Arras, together with other clerks of his diocese, to take action in the matter. They were authorized to force recalcitrant witnesses to testify by the application of ecclesiastical censures. The pope received further reports of the affair from clergy who convened at the Fourth Lateran Council of 1215. The relationship between the couple was computed and corroborated . by the testimony of various clerks in attendance at the council, and the allegation that Bochardus had been in orders was also confirmed by them.

The pontiff, convinced by the testimony he had heard at the council, "following the urge of piety in his innermost parts and wishing the duty of the pastoral office to be employed against the presumption of this nefarious rascal," ordered the Archbishop of Rheims and his suffragans to excommunicate Bochardus with bell and candle. On each Sunday and feast day the excommunication was to be proclaimed publicly throughout the regions where Bochardus might tarry with his illicit wife. The excommunication was to continue until the woman was restored to her sister, the Countess of Flan-

[5] *Ibid.*   [6] *Ibid.*

ders, and full restitution was made for damages the countess had suffered.[7] Bochardus also was to return "to honest conversion and the observation of the clerical order" before absolution would be accorded to him.[8] Innocent died before these coercive measures could operate, but his policy was continued by Honorius III (1216–1227).

The new pope in the first year of his pontificate renewed the censures against Bochardus. He declared that "divine piety which tolerated the man of iniquity arises from sleep and opens its closed eyes, so that it scrutinizes his iniquity and sees through the filth with which he is covered from the soles of his feet to the crown of his head." Bochardus was dubbed "an apostate who, immersed in deep slime, labors and clamors to the Lord that he deign to raise him from the lake of misery and the filth of putridity." The renegade priest, "his heart hardened, rotting in dung like a beast, with stiff neck closed his ears in the fashion of a deaf asp lest he hear discipline." [9]

Bochardus journeyed to Rome in an attempt to secure a dispensation which would enable him to remain in marriage with Margaret. His plea was refused, and he was directed to make a pilgrimage to the Holy Land to expiate his sin. After a year's sojourn at Jerusalem he returned and sought to rejoin his wife, but Countess Joanna would not permit Margaret to go to him.[10]

Termination of the case came with Margaret's submission. Forcibly separated from her lover, she petitioned the pope for absolution from the excommunica-

---

[7] *Ibid.*, 529, 530.　　　[8] *Ibid.*　　　[9] *Ibid.*, 530–31.
[10] Jacobus de Guisia, *Annales Hanoniae*, in *M.G.H., SS.*, XXX, 307.

tion which had been laid upon her some time after the pronouncement of the sentence on Bochardus. The absolution was extended in November, 1221, and Margaret was exhorted to give heed henceforth to her sister's salutary advice.[11] There is no record of absolution for Bochardus, and the two children born of this union were refused legitimacy by Gregory IX.[12]

After her absolution Margaret married William of Dampierre at her sister's insistence.[13] Here, too, relationship precluded a legitimate marriage, and Honorius ordered the dissolution of the union by a letter of November, 1223, on pain of excommunication.[14] The local clergy proved apathetic with the result that the pope wrote again in May, 1226, ordering steps to be taken to dissolve the marriage.[15] No action was taken in response to the papal mandates, and the death of William soon after obviated the necessity for continuance of papal interest.[16]

During the last years of Innocent's pontificate he intervened in a matrimonial case which was agitating the East. Erardus of Brienne contemplated marriage with the daughter of Henry, Count of Champagne, although she was related to him within the prohibited degrees.[17] Henry himself illegitimately had married Isabella, who, as the daughter of Sybil and Guido (Guy of Lusignan), was heiress to the Kingdom of Jerusalem. Isabella had been married before to Conrad

---

[11] *R.H.F.*, XIX, 716.   [12] Migne, *P.L.*, CCXVI, 535.

[13] Jacobus de Guisia, *Annales Hanoniae*, in *M.G.H.*, *SS.*, XXX, 307.

[14] *R.H.F.*, XIX, 738, 775.   [15] *Ibid.*, 775.

[16] *Biographie nationale de Belgique, sub* Burchardus de Avesnes (I, 558–63).

[17] Migne, *P.L.*, CCXVI, 941.

of Montferrat, who had been killed in 1192, and his
death was attributed to divine punishment for his incestuous marriage with her.[18] The daughter whom
Erardus wished to espouse was born of the marriage of
Isabella and Henry.[19] Innocent hastened to write to
Albert, Patriarch of Jerusalem, ordering him to prohibit the marriage under pain of excommunication, "lest
scandal arise from him from whom service ought to
come forth." At the same time he wrote to the bishops
of Soissons and Chalons, ordering them to excommunicate Erardus if he attempted to come to France with
the girl.[20]

The patriarch died soon after his receipt of the papal
instructions, and Erardus presumed to marry the girl
clandestinely before the elevation of Rudolph to the
patriarchal chair.[21] Innocent, ignorant of the secret marriage, wrote on February 20, 1213, to the new patriarch, reviewing the case. The pope declared that his
attention had been called to the case by Blanche, the
legitimate widow of Henry of Champagne and her son
Theobald, heir to the deceased count's dominions.[22]
They complained that Erardus had come to Jerusalem
to marry the deceased count's daughter so that he could
obtain the county of Tyre and other lands.[23] The widow
and her son, the rightful heir to his possessions, objected
to the marriage of Erardus, alleging that the couple
were related. They declared to the pope that the relationship was well known in France and they were prepared to prove it. Innocent recapitulated his previous
actions in the case and ordered the new patriarch to for-

[18] *Ibid.*, 976–77.   [19] *Ibid.*   [20] *Ibid.*, 941.
[21] *Ibid.*, 976.   [22] *Ibid.*, 973.   [23] *Ibid.*, 976.

bid the marriage.[24] He also ordered the Archbishop of
Caesarea to take similar action.[25]

Soon after the dispatch of these letters, the pope
learned of the clandestine marriage and Erardus' flight
from Jerusalem to Genoa, where he awaited a suitable
opportunity to go to France. The pope, assured of Philip
Augustus' support, wrote to the Bishop of Chartres and
other prelates, ordering them to compel Erardus to desist from his designs against Blanche and Theobald.[26]

Honorius continued his predecessor's policy. In his
first year he wrote to the French prelates renewing the
excommunication of Erardus. About the same time he
received assurances from Philip Augustus that Theobald would be allowed to hold the disputed lands under
the regency of his mother.[27]

In November, 1216, the pontiff received Blanche under his protection.[28] In December of the same year he
ordered ecclesiastical censures applied against supporters of Erardus.[29] The excommunication of Erardus was
reaffirmed in January, 1218, and all Christians were
cautioned against having any contact with him.[30] The
pope also ordered that energetic measures be taken to
quash his claims to lands belonging to Champagne.[31]

By December, 1218, Erardus seemed ready to comply with the papal mandates. The clergy of France
thereupon were directed to prepare to relax the sentences of excommunication and interdict which had been
promulgated against him from time to time, on condi-

[24] *Ibid.*, 973.   [25] *Ibid.*, 974.
[26] *Ibid.*, 976–77.   [27] *Ibid.*, 978, 982.
[28] A. Teulet (ed.), *Layettes du trésor des chartes* (Paris, 1863–1866),
I, 437, No. 1195.
[29] *R.H.F.*, XIX, 615, 618.   [30] *Ibid.*, 651.   [31] *Ibid.*, 649.

tion that he would prove ready to submit to all the papal demands.[32] Finally, on the twenty-ninth of December, the Abbot of Citeaux was instructed to grant absolution to the repentant sinner.[33]

The absolution was premature, for Erardus soon gave added offense to the papacy by laying waste much land in Champagne. Early in 1219 the pope ordered the clergy of Soissons to force him to desist from his spoliations and directed that he again be excommunicated if he did not prove amenable to their warnings.[34] He apparently again was excommunicated, for in July, 1219, the pope directed that absolution and Christian burial should be denied to all his partisans until adequate restitution were made to Blanche of Champagne for the damages she had incurred as a result of his depredations.[35]

About the same time the pontiff directed that the vassals of Erardus should be bound by oath to assist Blanche against his forces.[36] Blanche importuned the pope not to accord absolution until she had been compensated for the damages committed by him, and the pope made absolution contingent upon restitution.[37]

In November, 1219, deprivation was threatened against clerics who accorded Christian burial to followers of Erardus.[38] In October, 1220, the pontiff declared that

---

[32] *Ibid.*, 674.

[33] H. A. de Jubainville, *Histoire des ducs et des comtes de Champagne* (Paris, 1859), V, App., 143, No. 1173.

[34] *R.H.F.*, XIX, 675.

[35] Jubainville, *Histoire des ducs et des comtes de Champagne*, V, App., 143, No. 1215.

[36] *R.H.F.*, XIX, 689.   [37] *Ibid.*, 690.

[38] Jubainville, *Histoire des ducs et des comtes de Champagne*, V, App., 143, No. 1239.

absolution would be extended to Erardus and his followers if adequate recompense were given to Blanche for the damages she had sustained.[39] It is not known how peace was finally brought about, nor how much influence the attitude of the papacy had in allaying the strife. An agreement was made by which Erardus relinquished all claims on lands belonging to Blanche and Theobald, and the concordat was sanctioned by the pope in August, 1223.[40] With the political objectives attained, the question of the validity of the marriage was allowed to rest.

Enforcement from Honorius III to Boniface VIII

In addition to terminating marital cases in which the action was initiated by his predecessor, Honorius dealt with several other cases involving violations of the laws imposing the relationship impediments to marriage. On December 20, 1221, the pontiff ordered the Bishop of Limoges to prohibit the marriage of Raymond, a knight of Aubusson, with Margaret of the same place. An uncle of the girl had impugned the marriage and, finding the local clergy loath to take cognizance of the matter, had appealed to the pope.[41]

Honorius in March, 1222, ordered the Archbishop of York to take measures to dissolve the marriage of Alan, the constable of the King of Scotland, who was related to his wife within the forbidden degrees.[42] The same

---

[39] *R.H.F.*, XIX, 710.

[40] Migne, *P.L.*, CCXVI, 988; *Les registres de Grégoire IX, Bibliothèque des écoles françaises d'Athènes et de Rome*, Nos. 1240, 1241, 1735.

[41] *R.H.F.*, XIX, 717.

[42] A. Theiner (ed.), *Vetera Monumenta Hibernorum et Scotorum Historiam Illustrantia* (Rome, 1864), I, 20, No. 48.

pontiff also ordered the dissolution of the marriage of Guido of Castellione on the grounds that he and his wife, Agnes, were related within the proscribed degrees of consanguinity.[43]

There were also several instances of enforcement during the pontificate of Gregory IX. In February, 1229, Gregory ordered John, Bishop of Sabina, the papal legate in Spain, to dissolve the marriage contracted by the King of Aragon because of kinship between him and his wife.[44] The king was ordered to assign adequate revenues to support the erstwhile queen for the remainder of her life.[45] The same pontiff also prohibited the contemplated marriage of the daughter of the Count of Brittany and King Louis VIII of France (1223–1226).[46]

Innocent IV (1243–1254) intervened in an interesting case. The Marquis of Meissen, who had in wardship the daughter of Frederick II, conceived the plan of concluding a marriage alliance with the house of Hohenstaufen by having his son, Albert, marry the girl. The pope absolutely forbade the marriage and expressed surprise and disappointment that the marquis who hitherto had been an obedient son of the Church "wished to stain his house and posterity by his [Frederick's] evil blood." A legate of the Apostolic See then discovered, or claimed to discover, relationship between the prospective parties to the marriage and pronounced the sentences of excommunication and interdict on the marquis. The marquis hastened to explain that since the

[43] R.H.F., XIX, 738, 768.
[44] Les registres de Grégoire IX, Bibl. des écoles franc., No. 267.
[45] Ibid.; see Florez, España sagrada, XLIX, 167.
[46] Les registres de Grégoire IX, Bibl. des écoles franc., Nos. 87, 88.

couple were but two years old they were precluded from legitimate betrothal, and he eschewed any further designs to ally himself with Frederick II. The ecclesiastical censures were thereupon lifted.[47]

Pope Alexander IV (1254–1261) in 1256 ordered application of ecclesiastical censures against laymen of the diocese of Regensburg who were marrying their relatives and even presuming to dispute the teachings of the Church as to what constituted legitimate impediments to marriage.[48]

In 1283 Didacus, who had married Yolenda, the daughter of King Alfonso X of Castile and Leon (1252–1284), was ordered to separate from his wife on the grounds that they were related within the third degree of consanguinity.[49] The same year Pope Martin IV (1281–1285) ordered Sancius, the son of Alfonso X, to separate from his wife, Maria, because he was related to her within the third degree of blood relationship.[50] No further action was taken in these cases, so it is to be presumed that at least ostensible obedience was secured.

Celestine V in 1294 ordered Joseph, illegitimate son of King Peter IV of Aragon, to separate from his wife, a daughter of the King of Castile and Leon. The pope bewailed the prince's imprudence and contumacy and warned him that ecclesiastical censures would be inflicted if he did not promptly sunder the illicit union. The pontiff declared that any children which might be born

---

[47] J. L. A. Huillard-Bréholles (ed.), *Historia Diplomatica Friderici II* (Paris, 1852–1861), VI, Pt. I, 532, 534.

[48] *Les registres d'Alexandre IV, Bibl. des écoles franc.*, No. 1257; Potthast, *Regesta Pontificum Romanorum*, No. 16296.

[49] *Les registres de Martin IV, Bibl. des écoles franc.*, No. 304.

[50] Raynaldus, *Annales* (ed. Mansi), Ann. 1283, Pt. 57.

would be refused legitimacy and hence would be debarred from succession to their father's lands and honors. Nothing further was done in this case.[51]

In January, 1296, Boniface VIII (1294–1303) issued a decision in an important case. The Marquis of Montferrat had been betrothed to Blanche, daughter of King Charles of Sicily. The engagement was broken, and Blanche married James II, the king of Aragon. The marquis thereupon desired to marry Mary of Clermont, who was related to Blanche in the third degree and to the marquis in the same degree. Marriage of the marquis and Mary thus was barred because of the impediments of "public honesty" and consanguinity. The marquis endeavored to secure a dispensation, but Boniface informed him that the marriage positively would not be permitted.[52] The severity in this case was probably attributable to the fact that Blanche married the Aragonese ruler, who was in trouble with the pope over the question of the Sicilian throne as well as over the financial demands of the papacy in Aragon.[53]

Boniface also intervened in a case involving Curus and Texa of Florence. The pope forbade the marriage of the couple on the grounds that they were related within the fourth degree. He followed up his prohibition by a letter ordering them to refrain from carnal intercourse in the event that his earlier letter did not arrive in time to prevent celebration of the nuptials. If, however, the marriage had been consummated prior to the arrival of the papal prohibition, the pontiff directed that the par-

[51] *Ibid.*, Ann. 1294, App., 632.
[52] *Les registres de Boniface VIII, Bibl. des écoles franc.*, No. 886.
[53] H. Finke (ed.), *Acta Aragonensia* (Berlin, 1908), I, 55.

ties should perform adequate penance and refrain from sexual intercourse for a time, after which the local ecclesiastical authorities were empowered to grant them a dispensation to remain in wedlock.[54]

The same pontiff also forbade the contemplated marriage between James, son of the King of Aragon, and Isabella, the daughter of the King of Castile, because the relationship between the parties was so close as to preclude legitimate marriage.[55]

As has been shown there were relatively few cases of enforcement of the law subsequent to the pontificate of Innocent III. When our attention is turned to relaxations of the law, this same period affords an increasing number of examples where dispensations were accorded permitting marriage to be contracted within the forbidden degrees or granting leave to remain in marital relations contracted in violation of the law.

[54] *Les registres de Boniface VIII, Bibl. des écoles franc.*, No. 1077.
[55] *Ibid.*, No. 166.

CHAPTER IX

PAPAL POLICY AND RELAXATION OF THE LAW

EARLY INSTANCES OF DISPENSATION

AN early authentic instance of the exercise of papal clemency to remove an impediment to marriage engendered by relationship between the parties was the case involving William of Normandy and Matilda, daughter of Baldwin, Count of Flanders.

The exact relationship which precluded legitimate marriage between the couple is not clear. The most likely view is that the impediment was one of consanguinity, brought about by the relationship between Matilda's grandmother and Richard the Good of Normandy.[1] The prospective marriage was forbidden by an enactment of the Council of Rheims which was convoked by Leo IX (1048–1054), who journeyed into France to assemble the meeting in the interest of church reform.[2] It does not seem likely that any political motive actuated the pope in promulgating the prohibition; [3] his reforming zeal sufficiently accounts for his insistence on the enforcement of the canons.

No attempt seems to have been made to refute the

---

[1] E. A. Freeman, *The Norman Conquest* (London, 1875–1877), III, 650.

[2] Hefele, *Conciliengeschichte*, IV, 731.

[3] J. H. Ramsay, *The Foundations of England* (London, 1898), I, 491.

allegations of relationship, but the marriage took place in 1053 despite the papal prohibition.[4] Doubtless the difficulties of Leo in Italy strengthened William's resolve to flout the papal mandate.[5] The result of the defiance of the Holy See was that "by authority of the Roman Pope, all Neustria was suspended and interdicted from the service of Christianity." [6] Lanfranc censured William for his disobedience and was ordered into exile for his pains, but he was recalled when the duke encountered him as he was leaving his dominions with as much dispatch as his lamed steed allowed.[7]

Lanfranc made several trips to Rome in connection with the Eucharistic controversy which arose as a result of the writings and teachings of Berengar of Tours. On the occasion of his last visit he petitioned Nicholas II (1059–1061) to extend clemency to William. "Therefore, speaking with Pope Nicholas, he showed that the sentence injured them who neither joined them [in marriage] nor could separate them, since the duke did not wish to dismiss by any agreement the girl whom he had taken to wife. Hearing this and observing it to be true, the Highest Pontiff in the form of a dispensation allowed the marriage on condition that the duke and his wife construct two monasteries in which they were to establish single congregations of men and women respectively, who could there gain merit with God day and night under the rule of Holy Religion and plead for their salvation." [8] Under the terms of the dispensation William subsequently founded the House of St. Stephen

---

[4] *R.H.F.*, XI, 233, 246.

[5] Guillelmus Malmsburgensis, *De Gestis Regum Anglorum*, R.S., III, 267.

[6] *Vita Lanfranci* (ed. Giles), I, 288.   [7] *Ibid.*   [8] *Ibid.*

Proto-Martyr, while Matilda established the Convent of the Holy Trinity.[9]

The action of the pope was clearly a relaxation of the law since there was no question raised as to the validity of the charge that the couple were related. It will be noted that the dispensation was accorded, if we can believe the biographer of Lanfranc, on the grounds that compliance with the law could only be induced by the application of ecclesiastical censures which imposed hardship on innocent parties.

The papacy played but a minor part in the celebrated divorce of Louis VII of France (1137–1180). The activity of the pope during one phase of the marital litigation, however, really constituted a relaxation of the law. He not only permitted the couple to live together, although charges had been made that they were related within the forbidden degrees, but actually forbade their separation on the ground of relationship, and that aspect of the case merits attention.

The allegation of consanguinity apparently was first made by the Abbot of Clairvaux. The relationship was calculated by the Bishop of Laon. No separation seems to have been ordered by the local ecclesiastical authorities, nor did any such demand emanate from the Apostolic See. Louis was ardently devoted to his young wife whom he "loved in a puerile fashion," and hence naturally evinced no desire to separate from her even though strict compliance with the law would have made such action mandatory.[10]

Real trouble for the couple began while Louis was on

---

[9] *Gallia Christiana* (Paris, 1874), XI, 29, 31.
[10] *Historia Pontificalis*, in *M.G.H., SS.*, XX, 534.

his ill-fated crusade, on which project Eleanor insisted on accompanying him. When Louis wished to press on towards Jerusalem, Eleanor joined with her uncle, Raymond, Prince of Antioch, in an endeavor to induce her husband to prolong his sojourn within the walls of Antioch.[11] There the queen manifested undue attachment to her uncle, or at least simulated affection for him as a means to coerce her husband into postponing his projected march towards Jerusalem. As the chronicler informs us, "The familiarity of the prince with the queen and their continued and attentive conversation gave suspicion to the king which greatly disturbed him because the queen wished to remain there [Antioch]." [12]

While the disaffection was at its height, the queen revived the old charge of consanguinity.[13] Louis, much perturbed, was ready to separate from his troublesome wife, but Suger, by letter, advised him to defer action in the matter until he returned to France.[14]

On the way home from the crusade the royal couple, still estranged, met Eugenius III at Tusculum in October of 1149. The latter received the visitors with much honor and "appeased the discord of the king and queen which had begun at Antioch, after having heard the complaint of each, forbidding that mention be made of certain relationship between them and confirming the marriage both by word and writing. He forbade, under the prohibition of anathema, that anything important be heard or that the marriage be dissolved on any occasion."

[11] Guillelmus Neubrigensis, *Historia Anglicana*, R.S., I, 92.
[12] *Historia Pontificalis*, in *M.G.H., SS.*, XX, 534.
[13] Guillelmus de Nangiaco, *Chronica*, in *R.H.F.*, XX, 734.
[14] *R.H.F.*, XV, 509-10.

Louis was well pleased at the allayment of the marital difficulties, and the pope made haste to seal the reconciliation of the couple by "causing them to retire to the same bed, which he caused to be decorated with the most precious cloths." [15]

Louis again became jealous in 1152, and the marriage again was impugned on the grounds of consanguinity, this time at the behest of the king. A council was convoked at Beaugency in March, 1152, at which the union was pronounced dissolved.[16] There is no indication that the papacy played any part in the dissolution of the union, nor was there any effort made to enforce the previous dictum of the Holy See which pronounced anathema against anyone who attempted to institute proceedings against the marriage on the grounds of kinship. It is quite true that the silence of the pope might be construed as tantamount to consent to the separation, but there are no grounds for ascribing the failure of the pope to intervene to bribery of the cardinals.[17] Despite the importance of the divorce in the subsequent history of both France and England, Louis at the time of the separation gave little heed to possible consequences. Probably, "Eleanor so little concealed her affection for Henry that Louis lost his patience, and accorded obedience to false friends, more clever than he, who foresaw the lasting weakness of the kingly power by the irrevocable restitution of the dower of Eleanor in case of

[15] *Historia Pontificalis*, in *M.G.H., SS.*, XX, 537.

[16] *Historia Gloriosi Regis Ludovici VII, Coll. des textes*, IV, 163; Sigibertus, *Chronica*, in *M.G.H., SS.*, VI, 506.

[17] R. Hirsch, *Studien zur Geschichte König Ludwigs VII von Frankreich* (Leipzig, 1892), 80–81.

a separation, and, from selfishness, sought to hasten that event." [18]

There were several occasions during the pontificate of Alexander III when it seemed expedient or equitable to condone violations of the marital law dealing with the impediment of relationship. The pope in writing his response to inquiries of Gerard, Archbishop of Salonne, acting in the capacity of a papal legate, declared that although marriages had been contracted within the area of his jurisdiction in contravention to the law, he was to "pass over such marriages with silence and dissimulation because of the obduracy of the people, although they were against the institutions of the sacred canons." Nevertheless, the papal representative was ordered to take measures to prevent the contraction of such illicit unions in the future.[19]

In another instance the pontiff granted a dispensation where considerations of equity clearly dictated such action. A certain couple in the province of Rheims lived in marriage for more than ten years. Their marriage was then impugned by relatives on the ground that the couple were related within the forbidden degrees. It was represented to the pope that those relatives who lodged the information would benefit by the dissolution of the marriage since their share to a prospective inheritance would be considerably augmented. The pope in response to a petition ordered clemency to be extended to the suppliants if it might be done without stirring up scandal detrimental to the Church.[20]

---

[18] *Ibid.*   [19] Migne, *P.L.*, CC, 627–28.

[20] *Ibid.*, 544. For other cases in this pontificate, see Jaffé, *Regesta Pontificum Romanorum*, Nos. 13887, 14169.

Clement III issued an important decision wherein he authorized Jews and Saracens who had been converted to Christianity to remain with wives whom they had married prior to their conversion, even though consanguinity in the fourth degree ordinarily would have precluded such marriages. The contracting parties were not to be compelled to remain in uncanonical marital relations after their conversion, and if they elected to sunder the unions they were to be permitted to contract new marriages.[21]

RELAXATION OF THE MARITAL LAWS DURING THE PONTIFICATE OF INNOCENT III (1198–1216)

Innocent III, in his dealings with Otto of Brunswick (Otto IV), evinced a consistent readiness to condone violations of the marriage laws in the interests of peace and the furtherance of his anti-Hohenstaufen policy.

In December, 1200, the pope wrote to the Duke of Brabant in regard to a projected marriage between his daughter, Mary, and Otto. The pontiff declared that complaints had been made that the marital alliance was barred by consanguinity. He informed the duke, in order that "his conscience be not only cleansed but cheered," that "because of the great usefulness which we hope will be procured from this marriage," he should proceed at once to bestow his daughter on Otto with the sanction of the Holy See despite the impediment of consanguinity.[22] The marriage did not ensue, with the result that Innocent in March of 1202 confirmed his earlier permission for the nuptials and assured the duke

---

[21] Migne, *P.L.*, CCIV, 1493.   [22] *Ibid.*, CCXVI, 1022.

that he need have no qualms in regard to the validity of such a union.[23]

It soon appeared that the duke's reluctance to marry his daughter to the claimant to the German throne proceeded from reasons other than conscience. In a letter dated October, 1204, the pontiff chided the duke for his refusal to hand over his daughter to Otto. Frivolous reasons had been adduced to excuse the delay in complying with the papal wishes, whereas in reality the duke had been in correspondence with Philip of Swabia. Philip apparently induced the duke to betroth his daughter to Frederick, the infant son of the late Henry VI, and this project threatened to interfere not only with Innocent's plans for Otto's marriage but also with the marriage he had planned for Frederick with the sister of the King of Aragon. The pope informed the recalcitrant duke that he would not sanction the marriage of his daughter to Frederick and ordered him to bestow her hand on Otto without delay. The letter closed with thinly veiled threats of excommunication and interdict in the event of noncompliance with papal instructions.[24]

In September, 1205, the pontiff advised Otto to take matters into his own hands. The girl had not as yet attained the marriageable age, and Otto was counseled to wait until that time; then, if the girl's father still refused to hand her over to him, he was to "marry her fully in the Lord" without her father's consent.[25]

The marriage never took place, for the situation in Germany was abruptly changed by the murder of Philip

---

[23] *Ibid.*, 1073.   [24] *Ibid.*, 1114–16.
[25] *Ibid.*, 1128.

of Swabia in June, 1208.[26] Partisan bitterness was rampant, and the nobles considered what measures should be taken to allay it. "For this, nothing more suitable could be found than that King Otto take the daughter [Beatrice] of Philip in marriage since this would stabilize the concord between the king and princes by an indissoluble bond." However, this union "was not allowable without the Apostolic permission because kinship inhibited it, since the father of Otto was the relative of the late Emperor Frederick, who was the father of Philip." [27]

In order to overcome this impediment the Apostolic See was petitioned for a dispensation. In a letter dated August, 1208, Innocent wrote to the clergy of Germany declaring that it was his duty to pacify Germany. He exhorted the clergy to strive for peace, "consenting in the divine arrangement concerning our most dear son in Christ, Otto." The influential German clergy were ordered to facilitate the projected marriage.[28] In November of 1208 the proposed marriage was given further impetus. A diet was held at Frankfort, where Philip's daughter "was given to [Otto] in wardship with all the possessions which belonged to her from her ancestors." [29]

In December of the same year the pontiff wrote to Otto. He reviewed the requests for papal dispensation

---

[26] Heinricus Heimburgensis, *Annales*, in *M.G.H., SS.*, XVII, 713; *Ottonis Frisingensis Continuatio Sanblasiana*, in *M.G.H., SS.*, XX, 331.

[27] *Ottonis Frisingensis Continuatio Sanblasiana*, in *M.G.H., SS.*, XX, 332.

[28] Migne, *P.L.*, CCXVI, 1147-48.

[29] *Gesta Episcoporum Halberstadensium*, in *M.G.H., SS.*, XXIII, 122; *Annales Colonienses Maximi*, in *M.G.H., SS.*, XVII, 823.

and declared that "because you wished for this, as you intimated to us by your letter, we, from that special grace which we had and have for your person, after cautious deliberation, provided and committed to one or two of our legates whom we planned to send for the business of the Church and Empire, so that if urgent necessity or evident utility demands they shall dispense in the matter by our authority." [30]

Another letter was then sent to the German prelates. The pope set forth that he had labored with unmitigated zeal for the restoration of peace in the Empire since the schism imperiled both Germany and the world. "By wish of God, the Lord had restored tranquillity to the winds and sea, and many, returning to heart, adhered to the king so that there was a firmer hope for peace." The pontiff expressed his approval of the marriage to unite the two parties and authorized the king to proceed to marry Beatrice regularly "in the sight of the Church." [31]

A few days later the pope formally ordered his legates to grant a dispensation "if urgent necessity and evident utility for the restoration of peace in the Empire require it." [32] Two days later Otto was informed that the legates were on their way. [33]

The legates arrived in May, 1209; "coming to the king and greeting him with apostolic benediction, they revealed the cause of their legation . . . and extended him willingly the consent [for the marriage] for the defense of the Roman Church." [34] On May 24, 1209,

[30] Migne, *P.L.*, CCXVI, 1157.   [31] *Ibid.*, 1165.
[32] *Ibid.*, 1165–66.   [33] *Ibid.*, 1161.
[34] *Ottonis Frisingensis Continuatio Sanblasiana*, in *M.G.H., SS.*, XX, 333; *Annales Colonienses Maximi*, in *M.G.H., SS.*, XVII, 823.

a diet was convened at Herbolim.[35] The assembly was attended by most of the princes of Germany. Cardinal Hugh of Ostia, one of the legates, was asked to promulgate the pope's decision in regard to the marriage. He proclaimed the papal sanction in Latin, which the Bishop of Würzburg rendered into German for the benefit of Otto and the lay magnates.[36] Otto exhorted the legates to consider the matter carefully and declared that "if we lived for one thousand years we would rather live the celibate life than to consort with a wife in peril of our soul."[37] His scruples were overcome by the formal pronouncement of the legates who directed him to marry Beatrice "for good peace and concord and for wiping out the memory of the old evils."

There was some disaffection among the most strict clergy with the relaxation of the law even though papal dispensation had been accorded. We are informed that a Cistercian abbot arose and criticized the papal action and was supported by other Cistercian and Cluniac dignitaries. The disgruntled clergy were propitiated, however, by Otto's promise to perform works of charity to widows and orphans as penance. He also undertook to establish new Cistercian houses and to aid the projected crusade.[38]

After these matters were amicably adjusted, Beatrice was escorted into the assembly by Duke Leopold of

[35] *Ottonis Frisingensis Continuatio Sanblasiana,* in *M.G.H., SS.,* XX, 333; Arnoldus Lubecensis, *Chronica Slavorum,* in *M.G.H., SS.,* XXI, 247.
[36] *Ottonis Frisingensis Continuatio Sanblasiana,* in *M.G.H., SS.,* XX, 333.
[37] Arnoldus Lubecensis, *Chronica Slavorum,* in *M.G.H., SS.,* XXI, 247.
[38] *Ottonis Frisingensis Continuatio Sanblasiana,* in *M.G.H., SS.,* XX, 333.

Austria and Duke Ludwig of Bavaria. She was asked if she consented to the marriage, whereupon, "with bashfulness and profuse blushing," she manifested her assent. She was then "embraced by Otto and espoused by the public sign of a kiss and the presentation of rings." Otto thereupon turned to the assembly and bade them behold their queen.[39] The sacrament of marriage was not bestowed at this time, the mutual declaration of intent by both parties being considered sufficient to secure the recognition of Beatrice as queen. In July, 1212, however, when Otto's power was waning, he attempted partially to resuscitate it and to placate the truculent nobles by marrying Beatrice; she died about ten days after the ceremony.[40]

Innocent, by his readiness to condone infractions of the marriage laws when political expediency seemed to indicate the desirability of such a course, showed that "apostolic dispensation would be easy to obtain where political necessity spoke so loudly for it." [41]

There were other occasions during his pontificate when he deemed it advisable to dispense from the rigor of the marital laws. In 1204 he granted a dispensation to the Judge of Torres, who was related to his wife within the fourth degree. The couple were devoted to each other and were the parents of a son and two daughters. The judge, upon learning that he was related to his wife within the forbidden degrees, asked the pope for advice as to what course to pursue. Innocent, deprecating the scandal that would ensue if a separation were

---

[39] Arnoldus Lubecensis, *Chronica Slavorum*, in *M.G.H., SS.*, XXI, 247.

[40] Walterus de Coventria, *Memoriale, R.S.*, II, 204.

[41] E. Winkelmann, "Philipp von Schwaben und Otto IV," *Jahrbücher der Deutschen Geschichte, 1197–1208*, II, 505–506.

ordered, authorized the judge to remain in matrimony with his wife provided he had dismissed the concubines "which he had held according to the depraved custom of the land." [42]

Another case involved the Count of the Palace of Hungary. He married a noblewoman who was related to him in the second degree in ignorance of the fact that this relationship precluded the contraction of a legitimate marriage. Upon learning of his error and "making use of saner counsels," the count implored the pope for a dispensation. In support of his plea it was alleged that the couple had cohabited for many years without reproach and were the parents of several children. Representations were also made to the effect that grave scandal would arise were a separation demanded. In view of what he regarded as extenuating circumstances, the pontiff, in a letter of June, 1206, directed that a dispensation be granted if the facts as adduced by a more careful examination by the local ecclesiastical authorities coincided with the depositions which had been submitted to the Holy See. [43]

About the same time the pope wrote to the Archbishop of Torres (Turritano) in regard to the projected marriage of the daughter of the Judge of Cagliari to the Judge of Arbon. Rumors insinuated that the couple were related within the forbidden degrees. Innocent declared that great hopes were entertained for the peace of all Sardinia if this union and others of a similar nature were consummated. The archbishop was directed to proceed cautiously in the matter, and if a palpable impediment to the marriage were discovered the case was to

[42] Migne, *P.L.*, CCXV, 390–91.   [43] *Ibid.*, 894–95.

be submitted to Rome for final decision. Nothing further
was heard of the case; probably the allegations of relationship were not substantiated, and papal intervention was therefore unnecessary.[44]

The Duke of Austria in 1210, while preparing to go
on a crusade, gave his lands into the custody of the
Marquis of Meissen. To insure the good faith of the
custodian he wished to marry his son to the daughter
of the marquis. The couple were related within the
fourth degree; consequently a dispensation was sought
to legalize the projected union. In support of the petition for dispensation many nobles of Austria indicated
to the pope that much good would redound to the duchy
as a result of the marriage. In view of the beneficent
results anticipated by the Austrians, the pope in July
of 1210 authorized the Archbishop of Magdeburg, together with the Metropolitan of Salzburg, to accord the
desired relaxation of the canon law.[45]

Two years later the Count of Herve, through the
mediation of a procurator, asked the pope to stop the
inquiry which was being made as to the consanguinity
between him and his wife Matilda. The count was op-
pressing a neighboring monastery by undue procura-
tions, and the pope ordered measures to be taken against
him on this account, apparently without securing cessation of the spoliations. Consequently, when the petition
of the count in regard to the marital case came to the
Holy See, Innocent directed the Bishop of Paris and
other clergy to make the quashing of the marital proceedings contingent upon the count's agreement to desist from his illegal exactions from the monastery.[46]

---

[44] *Ibid.*, 897.   [45] *Ibid.*, CCXVI, 305.   [46] *Ibid.*, 602.

The pope wrote directly to the count in December of 1213. The pontiff declared that "he does not do injury if he dispenses, especially since a dispensation relaxes the chains of the law in some cases, where in others, it does not loose them, and so he extends them benefit of special grace which does not destroy the strength of the law in general." The count submitted to the pope's orders in regard to the monastery and, furthermore, vowed to assume the cross for a crusade, a declaration sure to secure pontifical favor. In return for his good conduct he received directly from the Holy See the desired dispensation legalizing his marriage.[47]

By the end of the pontificate of Innocent III precedents were well established for relaxing the application of the laws defining the impediments of relationship to marriage. Such dispensations were granted in the interest of papal policies, to insure peace, and to allay scandal. Concessions also were made where considerations of equity seemed to dictate such a course. After the time of Innocent III the number of dispensations multiplied, and they can be discussed to the best advantage if classified according to the ostensible motive that induced the exercise of papal clemency.

Relaxations of the Law in the Interests of Papal Policy (1216–1303)

During the thirteenth century there were many examples of dispensations accorded in marital cases wherein papal policies were served by granting the dispensations, or wherein the relaxations of the law served

[47] *Ibid.*, 943–44.

as rewards for previous devotion to the attainment of objectives of the Holy See.

Honorius III in August, 1223, granted a dispensation to the Emperor Frederick II so that he might marry Iolante, the daughter of the King of Jerusalem, who was said to be related to him within the fourth degree of consanguinity. The dispensation was granted in view of the projected crusade of the emperor, which he professed to be ready to undertake at that time, and it was thought that marriage to the daughter of the King of Jerusalem would be a means of "obligating him more firmly to this project." [48]

Gregory IX issued several dispensations which were justified on the grounds that the marriages therein permitted would be conducive to the restoration of tranquillity in the regions devastated by the ravages of the Albigensian crusade. In January, 1234, permission was granted to King Louis IX of France (1226–1270) to marry the daughter of Berengar, Count of Provence. The parties to the proposed union were alleged to be related within the fourth degree of kinship, but the pope declared that although "nothing but necessity induces dispensation" permission for the marriage was to be extended since "it profited the business of peace and faith for which so much labor and sweat had been expended." [49]

In January, 1228, Gregory gave permission for the marriage of Alfonso, brother of King Louis IX, and Johanna, the daughter of Raymond, Count of Toulouse.

---

[48] Huillard-Bréholles, *Historia Diplomatica Friderici II*, II, 394–95; Teulet, *Layettes du trésor des chartes*, II, 257, No. 2263.
[49] Raynaldus, *Annales*, Ann. 1234, Pt. 16.

Although the contracting parties were in this case also related within the fourth degree, the pope declared that he granted permission in the belief that thereby "he labored carefully for the restoration of peace between our most dear son in Christ, the illustrious King of the Franks, and Raymond, the son of the former Count of Toulouse," for the sake of "the good peace which we are held to covet as His vicar." [50] The pope also wrote to Alfonso, explaining that his legate had been instructed to grant the desired dispensation.[51]

Again, in connection with the late crusade against the heretics the pope accorded dispensations to William of Dampierre and Hugh of Castellione, who were related to their wives in the fourth degree of both consanguinity and affinity, because these two nobles had "helped, according to their means, in a creditable number of battles in the affair of the Albigenses." [52]

During the pontificate of Innocent IV the number of dispensations granted for reasons of policy was augmented by exigencies arising from the duel between the papacy and Frederick II. In March of 1244 Innocent ordered the Archbishop-elect of Cologne to grant dispensations to two noblemen who were related to their wives within the forbidden degrees because of the scandal and trouble that would ensue in the event of separation, but especially since "they had powerfully assisted in wars for the defense of the liberty of the Church." [53]

In the following month the pontiff dispensed for the

[50] C. Devic and J. Vaisette, *Histoire générale de Languedoc* (Toulouse, 1872–1905), preuves, VI, 630.

[51] Teulet, *Layettes du trésor des chartes*, II, 317.

[52] *Les registres de Grégoire IX*, Bibl. des écoles franc., No. 234.

[53] *Les registres d'Innocent IV*, Bibl. des écoles franc., No. 596.

benefit of the Landgrave of Thuringia, who married a woman related to him in the fourth degree of consanguinity, because the landgrave was "kindled by zeal for the Christian faith, and, with the inspiration of the Lord, was ardently striving in the defense of the catholic faith and the liberty of the Church." [54] In December of the same year Otto of Eberstein was the recipient of papal favor by which he was allowed to remain in marriage with a woman related to him within the forbidden degrees because he showed himself to be "prompt and devout in aid of this see." [55]

In July, 1245, Innocent conceded that the Lord of Maritania remain in marriage although he and his wife were related within the fourth degree because they "spontaneously offered eight knights, well armed, to be sent at their expense in aid of the Romans, which knights were devoted to the same through the space of one year." [56]

A certain G of Wassenberg received papal permission to remain in marriage with the widow of the Count of Cleves, even though the woman was related to him within the third degree of consanguinity. The pope admitted that scandal was likely to result from such a relaxation of the law, but declared that if the cause of Henry Raspe, the papal appointee to the imperial throne, were facilitated by the marriage, a dispensation was to be granted.[57] Again, in July, 1246, a dispensation was granted to Gerbert, Count of Stoltenbroke, who was married for eight years to a woman related to him within the fourth degree, because "the said count

[54] *Ibid.*, No. 600.   [55] *Ibid.*, No. 788.
[56] *Ibid.*, No. 1323.   [57] *Ibid.*, No. 2927.

offered himself and his family with his knights for maintaining and defending the justice of the Church, adhering to our most dear son in Christ, Henry Raspe, King
of the Romans." [58]

In August, 1247, the papal legate in Germany was instructed to grant dispensations to two knights, permitting them to remain in marriage with women who were
related to them within the proscribed degrees, "if you
think it aids in the business of the Church, and if they
align themselves against Frederick the Emperor." [59]

A dispensation was granted in September, 1248, to
Henry, a knight of Limberg, who married a woman related to another whom he had carnally known prior to
his marriage, thus engendering the impediment of affinity. The relaxation was granted because "the said
knight was said to labor faithfully in the cause of the
Church and in that of our most dear son in Christ, William, King of the Romans." [60]

With the pope now straining every nerve to secure
the recognition of William of Holland, designated King
of the Romans, as emperor, the number of dispensations
of all kinds was increased, and those applying to marital
cases were no exception. In December, 1248, the legate, Octavian, was ordered to grant a dispensation to
Ulric, son of the Duke of Carinthia, so that he might
marry Agnes, widow of the Duke of Austria, although
she was related to him within the third degree of affinity,
after suitable guarantees were received that the recipients of papal favor would assist against Frederick II.[61]

---

[58] *Ibid.*, No. 1996.   [59] *Ibid.*, No. 3231.   [60] *Ibid.*, No. 4168.
[61] A. Boczek (ed.), *Codex diplomaticus et epistolaris Moraviae*
(Prague, 1836–1864), III, 100, No. 132.

In January, 1251, the pontiff ordered that a dispensation be granted to Walter, a poor laic, enabling him to remain married to a relative. William, King of the Romans, requested that the dispensation be granted in that Walter "was of service to the said king in the business of the kingdom." [62]

Later in the same month cognizance was taken of a case involving Artimiannus, son of the Count of Froburc. A near relative of Artimiannus married a certain Anna, but before any carnal intercourse took place the marriage was annulled. Artimiannus then wished to marry Anna and applied for a dispensation. Although no affinity was engendered if there was no carnal consummation of Anna's first marriage, the relatively ill-defined impediment of "public honesty" precluded marriage unless papal action intervened. The pope ordered a dispensation to be granted "if it could be done without scandal and with the consent of our most dear son in Christ, William, King of the Romans." [63]

In February, 1251, a case occurred which well illustrates the length to which the pope was willing to go in order to secure the attainment of his paramount objective, the deposition of Frederick's heirs. A noblewoman, niece of the Bishop of Constance, petitioned the pope, declaring that she married a man who was related to her within the fourth degree of kinship. She explained that her husband would release captives he had taken and transfer his allegiance to the papal party if the pontiff would sanction the marriage. The pope re-

[62] J. Sbaralea (ed.), *Bullarium Franciscanum Romanorum Pontificum* (Rome, 1759–1768), I, 566, No. 358.
[63] *Les registres d'Innocent IV, Bibl. des écoles franc.*, No. 5004.

plied that if the conditions were fulfilled the couple were to be authorized to remain in marital relations.[64]

In July, 1252, Hugh, Cardinal Bishop of St. Sabina, a papal legate, was authorized to grant a dispensation to Buchard of Zigemberch permitting him to remain in marriage with his wife who was related to him within the fourth degree of consanguinity if he would deem it "expedient for the general business of the Church and the business of our most dear son in Christ, William." [65]

A few days later the same legate was ordered to grant a dispensation to a noble of Hainault, so that he might marry within the fourth degree, because "his help could be most fruitful to our most dear son in Christ, William, illustrious King of the Romans, and to the Roman Church." [66] In the same month a similar dispensation was accorded to a noble "because the said noble is devoted to the Roman Church and offers himself to . . . William, King of the Romans, in return for this kindness." [67] A dispensation was also granted to a certain Aegidius of Lyons because that city proved its devotion to the cause of William.[68]

In May, 1253, Innocent granted a dispensation to a certain Thomas who married a relative at the behest of Tancred, his father-in-law. The pontiff declared that he granted the dispensations "although the constitution

[64] *Ibid.*, No. 5074.

[65] J. Meerman, *Geschiednis van Graaf Willem van Holland, Roomsch Koning* (Gravenhaag, 1783–1797), Codex diplomaticus, No. 120.

[66] *Ibid.*, No. 121.

[67] T. Ripoll (ed.), *Bullarium Ordinis Fratrum Praedicatorum* (Rome, 1729–1740), I, 198, No. 236.

[68] *Ibid.*, 214, No. 262. See *ibid.*, 216–17, Nos. 267, 268 for similar cases.

of the sacred council [Fourth Lateran] forbade marriage to be consummated in the fourth degree of consanguinity or affinity, considering that the said Tancred is said to merit the grace and favor of this See by the effort of devout fidelity which he applied for the benefit of our legate, so that he sustained damages from enemies of the Church and is today deprived of one of his eyes." [69]

The son of Ottocar II, King of Bohemia, was granted permission to marry Margaret, Duchess of Austria, in July, 1253, although the contracting parties were related within a proximity sufficient to preclude marriage. It was set forth in the dispensation that the king and his son proved themselves devoted to the Holy See.[70] Shortly after instructing his legate to grant the dispensation, Innocent ordered him to refrain from announcing the concession until the prospective recipients of papal clemency avowed by oath their intention to aid William, King of the Romans. The king was to do liege homage to William if such acknowledgment were desired by him.[71]

In December, 1253, the pontiff set forth that "the sincerity of those devoted to the Church is now most powerfully augmented, since the bounty of the Apostolic See is discovered to be prompt and helpful." His legate was ordered to grant a dispensation to the widow of the Count Palatine of Tübingen, who married the Lord of Dwin ignorant of the fact that she was related to him within the fourth degree. Due consideration was to be taken of possible advantage to King William which

[69] Les registres d'Innocent IV, Bibl. des écoles franc., No. 6566.
[70] Sbaralea, Bullarium Franciscanum, I, 664, No. 486.
[71] Ibid., 665, No. 487. See Ripoll, Bullarium, I, 236, No. 308.

might ensue if papal clemency were exercised.[72] A few days later the same legate was empowered to grant dispensations relaxing the marital law to any five persons who because of gratitude for the indulgence of the pope might be helpful to the cause of King William.[73]

Other cases occurred during the time of Innocent IV in which dispensations were granted because of advantage to papal policy; but the details of those cases are similar to those already discussed and can be passed over without special attention.[74]

There were several instances of dispensations in marital cases during the time of Alexander IV which were in a measure involved in the struggle with Frederick and his heirs. In December, 1255, Alexander ordered Otto, Bishop of Brandenburg, to grant a dispensation to Conrad, son of the Margrave of Brandenburg, permitting him to marry his relative, Constantia, daughter of the Duke of Poland, on condition that the marriage would be pleasing to William, King of the Romans. It was also alleged that the marriage would be conducive to the establishment of peace between Brandenburg and Poland.[75]

The pope also issued a dispensation nullifying an impediment of kinship in the third degree which inter-

---

[72] Sbaralea, *Bullarium Franciscanum*, I, 688, No. 507. See *ibid.*, I, 670, No. 495; Meerman, *Geschiednis van Graaf Willem*, Codex diplomaticus, No. 225.

[73] Sbaralea, *Bullarium Franciscanum*, I, 705, No. 521.

[74] *Les registres d'Innocent IV, Bibl. des écoles franc.*, Nos. 1833, 1834, 4177, 4467, 6052, 7812; Meerman, *Geschiednis van Graaf Willem*, Codex diplomaticus, No. 187; Sbaralea, *Bullarium Franciscanum*, I, 715, No. 533; 721, No. 542.

[75] A. Theiner (ed.), *Vetera Monumenta Poloniae et Lithuaniae Gentiumque Finitimarum Historiam Illustrantia* (Rome, 1860), I, 60, No. 122.

posed between the Margrave of Brandenburg and the daughter of the Duke of Saxony. Alexander declared that the Holy See rarely granted a dispensation where the parties to a prospective marriage were related in the third degree, but "the prompt manifestations of aid and great services to the Church by the said nobles, especially in the business of William" were sufficient justification for the exercise of extraordinary clemency.[76] Alexander also confirmed several dispensations that had been issued by Innocent IV and alleged that service to King William, or general devotion to the policies of the Church, merited the kindness of the papacy.[77]

Several other papal objectives occasionally were served by the granting of marital dispensations. In March, 1259, Alexander IV was asked to permit the marriage of Waldemar, King of Sweden, to Sophia, niece of the King of Denmark, although the parties were related within the third degree of consanguinity. The pontiff acceded to the request and declared that he did so because it was hoped that the contemplated marriage would induce better co-operation between Sweden and Denmark in repulsing the pagans from the borders of Sweden.[78]

The papal effort to secure the Sicilian throne for Charles of Anjou was also involved in several matrimonial dispensations. In May, 1264, Urban IV (1261–1265) ordered his legate, Simon, Cardinal Priest of St. Caecilia, to dispense for any five persons in France,

---

[76] Ripoll, *Bullarium*, I, 282, No. 28.

[77] *Les registres d'Alexandre IV*, Bibl. des écoles franc., Nos. 501, 2123; Theiner, *Vetera Monumenta Hibernorum*, I, 82, No. 216.

[78] Sbaralea, *Bullarium Franciscanum*, II, 328, No. 475.

permitting them to contract marriages with relatives in the fourth degree or to remain in such unions if already concluded, so that he might "more efficiently promote the business of the King of Sicily." [79] A few days later the legate received authorization to accord similar favors to any four persons.[80] A considerable number of dispensations to individuals were also granted in connection with the establishment of Charles as king of Sicily.[81]

Clement IV (1265–1269) followed the practice of his predecessor. In March, 1265, he ordered that dispensations be granted to any four persons, in order that the attainment of the Sicilian objective might be facilitated. In November, 1267, the pontiff wrote to Charles: "In order that your situation may be stabilized on all sides, you may marry your children of either sex to persons who are related to them in the fourth degree of consanguinity or affinity." [82]

Attempts to strengthen and extend the Latin Kingdom of Jerusalem, together with the perennial, abortive projects for a general crusade, were in several instances the ostensible motives that impelled the popes to condone marriages in contravention to the canons. Gregory IX granted a marital dispensation on condition that its recipient would devote one third of his total revenues for a period of three years for the benefit of the Holy Land.[83] In 1265 Clement IV authorized the King of Cyprus, heir to the Kingdom of Jerusalem, to marry his

---

[79] Martène, *Thesaurus Anecdotorum*, II, 65.
[80] *Les registres d'Urbain IV, Bibl. des écoles franc.*, No. 624.
[81] *Ibid.*, Nos. 464, 576, 831.
[82] Martène, *Thesaurus Anecdotorum*, II, 537.
[83] *Les registres de Grégoire IX, Bibl. des écoles franc.*, No. 3080.

relative on the grounds that the marriage would secure the allegiance of a powerful protector for the kingdom.[84] The King of Armenia received papal permission to marry a relative in the fourth degree since it was hoped that the union would "bear an increase of usefulness to the Holy Land." [85]

Gregory X (1271–1276) declared that his relaxation of the law by which King Philip III of France was permitted to marry Queen Blanche of Navarre was justified by the fact that aid was promised for the Holy Land if the marriage were allowed. He also expressed the hope that the union would allay domestic discord that dissipated military strength which might be used with more propriety to the advantage of the Kingdom of Jerusalem.[86] In 1274 the same pontiff authorized his legate in France to concede dispensations relaxing the marriage laws for any four persons whom he might deem disposed to grant aid for the Holy Land.[87]

Nicholas III sanctioned the marriage of a certain Thomas who was related to his wife in the fourth degree because it was alleged that he "was prepared to aid the Holy Land in the next general crusade." [88] In May, 1286, Honorius IV (1285–1289) issued a dispensation legalizing marriage between children of the King of Cyprus and the King of Armenia since the intermarriage of the two houses would be beneficial to the Christian cause in Palestine.[89] Nicholas IV (1289–1292) re-

---

[84] Martène, *Thesaurus Anecdotorum*, II, 135.
[85] *Ibid.*, 293.
[86] *Les registres de Grégoire X, Bibl. des écoles franc.*, Nos. 873–77.
[87] *Ibid.*, No. 567.
[88] *Les registres de Nicholas III, Bibl. des écoles franc.*, No. 493.
[89] *Les registres de Honorius IV, Bibl. des écoles franc.*, No. 512.

laxed the marital laws in favor of the sister of the King
of Cyprus and the son of the King of Armenia because
as a result of the marriage it was hoped that "much
utility would redound to the Holy Land, together with
more security to the faithful dwelling in those regions." [90]

Occasionally, more trivial policies were involved in
according marital dispensations. Nicholas IV in permitting the marriage of Henry, Count of Luxemburg,
to Margaret, daughter of Duke John of Brabant, made
the dispensation contingent upon the cessation of the
spoliations which the duke was perpetrating on the
churches within his lands.[91]

The attainment of papal objectives was in many instances the motive for according dispensations relaxing
the rigor of the marital laws. In addition, dispensations
were also granted to kings and other important persons
whose devotion the popes were anxious to secure even
where no specific phase of papal policy was involved
in the case.

In August, 1237, Gregory IX granted Philippa, the
daughter of the Count of Poitou, permission to marry
Alfonso, son of the King of Castile and Leon, although
it was alleged that relationship sufficiently close to prevent marriage existed between the parties.[92] Philippa
had been married by proxy to Henry III, King of England, but the marriage had been nullified upon allegation that consanguinity in the forbidden degrees existed
between the parties.[93]

[90] *Les registres de Nicholas IV, Bibl. des écoles franc.*, No. 2667.
[91] *Ibid.*, No. 5864.
[92] *Les registres de Grégoire IX, Bibl. des écoles franc.*, No. 3849.
[93] T. Rymer (ed.), *Foedera et Acta Publica* (London, 1816), I, Pt.

At the request of Louis IX of France, Gregory also granted a dispensation to Robert, brother of the king, enabling him to marry Matilda, daughter of Henry II, Duke of Lorraine and Brabant. It was reported that the couple were related within the proscribed degrees, and the dispensation was secured as a precaution against subsequent questioning of the marriage.[94]

Innocent IV issued a dispensation permitting King James I of Aragon (1213–1276) to marry his son to any noblewoman, even though she might be related to him within the fourth degree, and a similar concession was made for the benefit of any one of the king's daughters.[95] In 1249 the king was again the recipient of papal favor. He wished to marry his daughter, Yola, to Alfonso, eldest son of King Alfonso IX of Castile, but the marriage was illegal because Alfonso had enjoyed carnal intercourse with a near relative of Yola. The pope granted a dispensation nullifying the impediment of affinity and permitted the couple to marry.[96]

In August, 1250, Leonore, the daughter of the King of Castile, received papal permission to marry any nobleman, even though her prospective husband might be related to her within the fourth degree.[97] In 1251 similar concessions were made to the children of the King of Aragon.[98] The King of Portugal was the recipient of papal clemency in 1252 when a dispensation

---

I, c. 129, 130; *Les registres de Grégoire IX, Bibl. des écoles franc.*, Nos. 3847, 3155.

[94] *Ibid.*

[95] *Les registres d'Innocent IV, Bibl. des écoles franc.*, No. 1802.

[96] Baluze, *Miscellanea*, I, 217.

[97] *Les registres d'Innocent IV, Bibl. des écoles franc.*, No. 4782.

[98] Raynaldus, *Annales*, Ann. 1251, Pt. 30.

authorized him to remain in marriage with his wife, who was related to him within the forbidden degrees.[99]

In 1254 the son of the Queen of Navarre received a dispensation sanctioning his marriage with any noble-woman whom he might select, even though she were related to him within the fourth degree.[100] About the same time a dispensation was issued permitting marriages among certain related nobles in Denmark. The dispensation was procured at the intercession of King Waldemar.[101]

Similar concessions were made to nobles who were not members of royal families. In 1246 Innocent IV, in answer to a petition of Simon de Montfort, granted a dispensation authorizing one of the count's retainers to remain in marital relations with a woman related to him within the forbidden degrees.[102] In the same year a son of the Countess of Flanders received permission to contract marriage with a relative.[103] Again, in 1247 a vassal of Simon de Montfort was permitted to remain married to a woman who was related to him in a degree sufficiently close to preclude marriage, and the count's petition was instrumental in securing the desired relaxation of the law.[104] In 1253 a certain Caecilia received permission to marry any noble whom she might choose, even though he were related to her within the fourth degree. The dispensation was promulgated because the woman was a niece of the Archbishop of Magdeburg,

---

[99] Sbaralea, *Bullarium Franciscanum*, I, 632, No. 441.

[100] Martène, *Thesaurus Anecdotorum*, I, 1058.

[101] J. Liljegren (ed.), *Svenskt Diplomatarium* (Stockholm, 1829–1867), I, 357, No. 397. See *ibid.*, II, 87, No. 1009 for a similar case.

[102] *Les registres d'Innocent IV, Bibl. des écoles franc.*, No. 1729.

[103] *Ibid.*, No. 1839.   [104] *Ibid.*, No. 2791.

who petitioned the pope in her behalf.[105] The Count of
Flanders received a dispensation in 1254 which allowed
him to marry any two of his children to nobles who
might be related to them within the fourth degree.[106]
Very probably, noble families found it increasingly difficult to arrange marriages with persons of proper rank
who were not related to them within the forbidden degrees, so that considerations of equity justified relaxation of the law; but the letters of dispensation expressly
stated that special consideration was to be extended because of the "quality of the persons" involved in these
cases.

Similar cases occurred after the death of Innocent IV.
Alexander IV granted a matrimonial dispensation because King Alfonso X of Castile requested him to do
so.[107] Clement IV in 1265 permitted Henry, brother of
the King of Navarre, to marry any noblewoman, even
though she were related to him within the forbidden degrees. Only the daughters of Simon de Montfort, who
was in disfavor with the Holy See because of his rebel-
lion against Henry III of England, were excepted.[108]
In 1263 Urban IV legalized the marriage of King Alfonso of Portugal to Beatrice, who was related to him
within the fourth degree, on the grounds that since the
kingdom was a fief of the Holy See the pope might
exercise clemency in matters which might conduce to the
benefit of his vassal.[109]

[105] Ripoll, *Bullarium*, I, 222, No. 281. See *Les registres d'Innocent IV*,
Bibl. des écoles franc., No. 3480 for a similar case.
[106] *Les registres d'Innocent IV, Bibl. des écoles franc.*, No. 7582.
[107] *Les registres d'Alexandre IV, Bibl. des écoles franc.*, No. 861.
[108] Martène, *Thesaurus Anecdotorum*, II, 124–25.
[109] *Les registres d'Urbain IV, Bibl. des écoles franc.*, Nos. 375, 376.

CHAPTER X

RELAXATION IN THE INTEREST OF PEACE AND EQUITY

THE desire of the popes to establish peace between warring Christian countries and the wish to minimize private warfare were often the motives for granting dispensations in matrimonial cases.

During the pontificate of Honorius III the marriage of Otto, grandson of King Waldemar of Denmark, and a daughter of Margrave Albert of Brandenburg was permitted on the grounds that the intermarriage of the houses would serve "to allay the wars and pestilences induced by the enmity between Denmark and Brandenburg."[1]

In 1238 Gregory IX approved the marriage of the Duke of Pomerania to a niece of King Waldemar of Denmark, although the parties were related within the forbidden degrees, because the marriage was for the ostensible purpose of "allaying the chief enmities between the Danes and the Slavs which arose from sinful demands and for the restoration of treaties affecting them."[2]

Eric, the son of the Danish sovereign, received papal permission to marry Iutta, a daughter of the Duke of

---

[1] A. F. Riedel (ed.), *Codex Diplomaticus Brandenburgensis* (Berlin, 1838–1869), II, Pt. I, 190, No. 246.

[2] P. Suhm, *Historie af Danemark* (Copenhagen, 1782–1828), IX, 772.

Saxony, who was related to him within the fourth degree. The dispensation was granted because between
Denmark and Saxony "grave discord had arisen, and
because of this, much slaughter of men, desolation of
lands, and grave perils to souls had been incited." It
was hoped that the marriage would facilitate the restoration of peaceful relations.[3] Waldemar himself received
papal permission to marry a niece of the Duke of Pomerania on the plea that such a marriage would stabilize
the peaceful relations of the Danes and Slavs.[4]

In 1262 Ottocar II, King of Bohemia, petitioned the
pope to legitimate his *de facto* union with Kunigunda,
who was related to him within the fourth degree of
consanguinity and the third degree of affinity. Ottocar
was canonically separated from his former wife, Margaret, who had entered a nunnery, so that relationship
was the only impediment to his marriage to Kunigunda.
Urban IV granted a dispensation because the marriage
was considered a means to preserve peace between Poland and Hungary.[5]

Martin IV in 1284 conceded permission to Elena, a
relative of the King of Sweden, to marry a nobleman
who was related to her in the fourth degree in order
to appease domestic strife in the Kingdom of Sweden.[6]
In order to safeguard peaceful relations the pontiff also
permitted the marriage of Birgero, son of King Magnus
of Sweden, to a daughter of King Eric of Denmark al-

[3] *Ibid.*, 773.   [4] *Ibid.*, 772.
[5] Boczek, *Codex diplomaticus et epistolaris Moraviae*, III, 332.
[6] Raynaldus, *Annales*, Ann. 1284, Pt. 23; Liljegren, *Svenskt Diplomatarium*, I, 649, No. 697.

though consanguinity would have ordinarily precluded their marriage.[7]

Edward I of England and his family were in several instances the recipients of papal favor in marital cases on the grounds that relaxations of the severity of the marital laws would serve the cause of peace and order. In November, 1289, Edward, the son of the king, petitioned the pope to sanction his proposed marriage to Margaret, daughter of Eric of Norway and granddaughter of the King of Scotland. It was pointed out that "because of the nearness of England and Scotland, divers scandals, rancors, and hatreds are begotten between the two realms and their kings from which, as it is learned, perils to bodies and goods are imminent." It was explained that Margaret was heiress to the Scottish throne, and Edward desired to marry her "for the procuring and nourishing of the benefits of true peace and affection between the said kingdoms and their inhabitants." The parties were related in the third degree, but Nicholas IV, in view of the hopes for peace that were entertained, and considering that Edward I because of this peace might be free to go to the Holy Land on a crusade, granted a dispensation and legitimated in advance any children which might be born to the couple.[8] Margaret's tragic death on the way to her betrothed and the political complications thereby induced are well known and beyond the scope of this work.

Two years later Nicholas acquiesced in the request

---

[7] Raynaldus, *Annales*, Ann. 1284, Pt. 24.

[8] Rymer, *Foedera et Acta Publica*, I, Pt. III, c. 57.

that he sanction the proposed marriage of young Edward and Blanche, daughter of Philip the Fair. The couple were related within the third degree, but the pontiff pointed out that this was an occasion wherein the dispensing power of the Holy See could be used with propriety, "hoping that if a particle of rancor still remained between France and England it might be removed by the consummation of this marriage." Nicholas also declared that Edward I was a pledged crusader, and stabilization of peace between the two kingdoms would accelerate the proposed expedition and enhance the chances of its success.[9]

This projected marriage also failed to materialize, but in July, 1298, Edward I received from Boniface VIII a dispensation authorizing his son's marriage to Isabella, another daughter of Philip IV. Here too relationship ordinarily would have precluded the union, but the pope, calling attention to "the disorders of war, the tempests of scandal, the blowings of turbulence, and the tempests of conflict in which the spirit of Satan, jealous of peace, had embroiled both kingdoms," declared that the marriage would largely obviate the danger of a recurrence of such conditions.[10]

Philip IV in October, 1300, received permission for the marriage of his son, Louis, to Margaret, daughter of Robert, Duke of Burgundy. The pontiff disavowed any selfish designs in condoning a marriage which kinship impeded but declared that he acted solely "for the sake of the kingdom of France and its inhabitants and

---

[9] *Les registres de Nicholas IV, Bibl. des écoles franc.*, No. 7376.
[10] *Les registres de Boniface VIII, Bibl. des écoles franc.*, No. 2626.

for restoring it to a good and peaceful condition." [11]

In addition to utilizing matrimonial dispensations to procure peaceful relations among warring principalities, the canons often were relaxed to mitigate private warfare between noble houses or to compose the differences that were responsible for such outbreaks. Innocent IV ordered the Archbishop of Cologne to annul the impediment of consanguinity which interposed between Matilda, the daughter of the Duke of Brunswick, and the Margrave of Brandenburg. The Count of Anehalt intimated to the pope that a quarrel had broken out between his father and the margrave, and the enmity could not be allayed unless the proposed marriage were concluded. [12]

In July, 1253, the pope permitted the marriage of a son of the Marquis of Meissen to Agnes, daughter of the Margrave of Brandenburg, in order to establish peaceful relations between the two houses, although it was known that the parties were related in the fourth degree of consanguinity. [13] Two years later Alexander IV legalized the marriage of Albert, another son of the marquis, to Agatha, another daughter of the margrave, on the grounds that the marriage would be an additional guarantee of peace. [14] Alexander also authorized the marriage of Conrad, a son of the margrave, to Constantia, daughter of the Duke of Poland, who was related to him within the forbidden degrees since "it was hoped that peace and concord would ensue between

[11] *Ibid.*, No. 3724.
[12] Riedel, *Codex Diplomaticus Brandenburgensis*, II, Pt. I, 25, No. 37.
[13] *Ibid.*, 41, No. 60.　　　　[14] *Ibid.*, 43, No. 63.

the said duke and margrave; murder would be avoided, and quiet and tranquillity procured in those regions." [15] In 1256 the pope sanctioned the marriage of the daughter of the chamberlain of the King of Bohemia to a nobleman who was related to her. The dispensation was granted ostensibly to terminate quarrels.[16]

Gregory X in 1275 vouchsafed approval of the marriage of John, son of Henry of Hastings, and Isabella, daughter of the Earl of Pembroke, a brother of Henry III of England. Although the parties were alleged to be related within the proscribed degrees, the pope granted a dispensation in view of the fact that "the said Henry opposed himself hostilely to the said King Henry in the time of disturbance in the kingdom," and it was hoped that the marriage would allay the disaffection.[17]

Nicholas III (1277–1281) ordered the chapter of Brandenburg to dispense in favor of Henry, Lord of Slavia, so that he might marry Beatrice, daughter of Albert, Margrave of Brandenburg, despite the impediment of consanguinity. The dispensation was granted because it was hoped that the marriage would insure peace, and the matter was committed to the chapter because of a vacancy in the see.[18]

In 1286 Honorius IV ordered the Bishop of Hereford to concede the Lord of Clifford permission to marry Margaret of Newburgh, who was related to him

---

[15] Theiner, *Vetera Monumenta Poloniae*, I, 60, No. 122.

[16] Sbaralea, *Bullarium Franciscanum*, II, 178, No. 259. See *ibid.*, III, 344, 368, 403.

[17] Rymer, *Foedera et Acta Publica*, I, Pt. II, c. 149.

[18] Riedel, *Codex Diplomaticus Brandenburgensis*, II, Pt. I, 200, No. 256.

within the fourth degree. The marriage was challenged by some who alleged that the couple were related, but the pope granted the dispensation on the grounds that the union was conducive to peace.[19]

Gilbert, Count of Hereford, in 1289 was granted papal sanction for his proposed marriage to Johanna, daughter of Edward I, even though it was alleged that kinship existed between the couple. The pontiff held that the interests of peace would be served by indulgence in the application of the law.[20] Nicholas IV also conceded authority to Waldemar, Prince of Denmark, to marry his relative, a daughter of the late Duke John of Saxony, in order to obviate the possibility of a recurrence of the parental discords.[21]

In 1302 Boniface VIII allowed Humphrey, Count of Hereford, to marry a widowed daughter of Edward I, although the parties were related within the third degree of affinity and the fourth degree of consanguinity. It was alleged that the union would strengthen the friendship of the two houses.[22]

He also authorized Margrave Henry of Brandenburg to remain in marriage with a daughter of the Duke of Bavaria, although the marital canons were contravened, because the marriage was considered an influence for the preservation of peace.[23] For the same reason he legitimated the marriage of Eberhard, Count of

---

[19] Rymer, *Foedera et Acta Publica*, I, Pt. III, c. 6.

[20] *Ibid.*, c. 57.

[21] H. F. Rördam (ed.), *Ny kirkehistoriske Samlinger* (Copenhagen, 1864), III, 384, No. 68. See *ibid.*, 390, 393 for similar cases in Scandinavia.

[22] Rymer, *Foedera et Acta Publica*, I, Pt. IV, c. 17.

[23] Riedel, *Codex Diplomaticus Brandenburgensis*, II, Pt. I, 251, No. 319.

Wittenberg, to Matilda, daughter of the Count of Hohenberg.[24]

Beginning with Innocent IV it is found that the papal court issued a large number of dispensations as matters of routine, and the reason which was given for these relaxations of the law was that the interests of peace were served. A set formula was used with but few deviations, and it is quite unlikely that the popes personally interested themselves in these cases. For the most part these dispensations were disseminated by the Friars, and there apparently was no legatine examination of the facts alleged as justification for the exercise of papal clemency. Geographically, the dispensations were granted to individuals all over Christian Europe. A number of persons with no titles of nobility were the recipients of such dispensations.[25]

DISPENSATION IN THE INTEREST OF EQUITY

A number of marital dispensations were granted where extenuating circumstances justified such conces-

[24] J. Kopp, *Geschichte der eidgenössischen Bünde* (Vienna, 1851), Urkunden, III, 325.

[25] *Les registres d'Innocent IV*, Bibl. des écoles franc., Nos. 1345, 1400, 1408, 1447, 1633, 4511, 4771, 4891, 4896, 4959, 5130, 5265, 5475, 5999, 6245, 6473, 6896, 7351, 7904; *Les registres d'Alexandre IV,* Bibl. des écoles franc., Nos. 294, 371; *Les registres d'Urbain IV, Bibl. des écoles franc.,* No. 86; *Les registres de Nicholas III, Bibl. des écoles franc.,* No. 88; *Les registres de Martin IV, Bibl. des écoles franc.,* No. 35; *Les registres de Honorius IV, Bibl. des écoles franc.,* No. 232; *Les registres de Nicholas IV, Bibl. des écoles franc.,* Nos. 178, 182, 184, 266, 325, 383, 408, 444, 476, 488, 490, 665, 765, 816, 858, 872, 1027, 1076, 1270, 1279, 1356, 1625, 1650, 1755, 1759, 1814, 1985, 2276, 2466, 2601, 2618, 2652, 2653, 2665, 2666, 2855, 2891, 2900, 3189, 3293, 3340, 3972, 3986, 4097, 4150, 4784, 4915, 5044, 5128, 5460, 5579, 5756, 6095, 6173, 6181, 6284, 6341, 6362, 6381, 6396, 6403,

sions from considerations of equity. In 1237 Gregory IX
ordered that the Viscount of Cardona be permitted to
remain in marriage with his wife, whom he married
many years before ignorant of any relationship between
them. When the couple learned that they were related,
they petitioned for a dispensation to legitimate their
union. The pontiff directed that the dispensation be
granted if it could be done without inciting scandal, and
if the viscount would agree to furnish forty knights for
a year's service against the Moors in Spain.[26]

During the rule of Innocent IV a certain Peter of
Verino requested a dispensation authorizing him to remain in marriage. He and his wife had secured permission to marry from a certain archdeacon, although it was
known that a former husband of the woman was related to Peter. After they had lived together for three
years, a priest who disliked them reopened the case by
impugning the marriage on the grounds that affinity
existed. A new archdeacon, before whom the case was
brought, ordered the marriage nullified, but the parties appealed to the Holy See for a dispensation. In view
of the extenuating circumstances involved in the case,
Innocent permitted them to remain in marital relations.[27]

This pope also intervened in another interesting case.
A certain Ulric married one Christina and begot several
children by her. After several years of connubial felic-
ity Ulric became embroiled in an altercation with his

6431, 6437, 7105; *Les registres de Boniface VIII, Bibl. des écoles franc.*,
Nos. 239, 245, 325, 365, 509, 605, 615, 617, 1146, 1275, 1339, 1342,
1429, 1460, 1777, 2513, 2659, 2817, 3016.

[26] Ripoll, *Bullarium*, I, 91, No. 159.

[27] *Les registres d'Innocent IV, Bibl. des écoles franc.*, No. 1191.

brother-in-law and slew him. Then a report was circulated that the marriage was illegal since spiritual relationship existed between the couple. The pope ordered that the marriage be considered legitimate since the parties were ignorant of any relationship. It was also represented to the pope by the Bishop of Ratisbon that the hatred engendered by the murder would subside more quickly if the marriage were not nullified, and this consideration also impelled the pope to extend clemency.[28]

Honorius IV authorized relaxation of the marital law in favor of Ioffredus, who unwittingly married in contravention to an impediment of "public honesty." He was betrothed to a girl who subsequently embraced the celibate life, thus dissolving the betrothal. He then married a relative of his first betrothed, ignorant of the fact that the annulment of his first betrothal did not remove the impediment of "public honesty" which prevented him from marrying a relative of the woman to whom he once had been engaged. Because of the quite understandable ignorance of the petitioner as to the provisions of the law, the pope issued the desired dispensation.[29]

Ignorance of the law, while doubtless originally a bona fide justification for its relaxation, soon became merely a nominal reason for the large number of routine dispensations which were issued by the papal court.[30]

[28] *Ibid.*, No. 7633. See *ibid.*, No. 6823 for a similar case.

[29] Sbaralea, *Bullarium Franciscanum*, III, 581, No. 60.

[30] *Les registres d'Innocent IV, Bibl. des écoles franc.*, Nos. 4296, 4785, 5051, 5712, 6462, 6533, 7052; *Les registres de Honorius IV, Bibl. des écoles franc.*, Nos. 259, 268, 273, 458; *Les registres de Nicholas IV, Bibl. des écoles franc.*, Nos. 411, 453, 489, 664, 805, 829, 909, 951, 1044, 1062, 1073, 1137, 1138, 1139, 1300, 1305, 1313, 1315, 1451, 1454, 1564, 1586, 1657, 1662, 1722, 1725, 1760, 1818, 1983, 1986,

The obvious difficulty of securing conjugal mates of proper station who were not relatives within the forbidden degrees was responsible for several dispensations which may be classified as concessions to considerations of equity.

Innocent IV authorized marriages of relatives in the fourth degree of consanguinity among the Christians in North Africa because their relatively limited number made it difficult to contract marriages without violating the law.[31] The pope also granted dispensations to the nephews of the Duke of Burgundy since they were unable to find suitable brides who were not related to them within the proscribed degrees.[32] In 1290 Urban IV permitted the Patriarch of Jerusalem to dispense for the benefit of any ten nobles in his jurisdiction, so that they might marry women who were related to them within the fourth degree "because of the scarcity of the faithful who are in the regions of the Holy Land."[33]

CONCLUSIONS

The Christian legislation imposing the impediments of relationship to marriage derived its precedents from the Roman law and the Scriptures. The Roman law for-

---

2001, 2003, 2004, 2012, 2096, 2112, 2135, 2321, 2354, 2611, 2672, 2681, 2707, 2757, 2821, 2824, 2867, 2868, 2886, 2911, 3032, 3041, 3079, 3104, 3113, 3182, 3249, 3250, 3293, 3342, 3346, 3347, 3368, 3454, 3686, 3779, 3784, 3791, 3826, 3828, 3956, 4030, 4095, 4474, 4554, 4555, 4612, 4681, 4682, 4683, 4686, 4689, 4690, 4860, 4888, 5110, 5111, 5127, 5344, 5586, 5621, 5975, 6029, 6051, 6052, 6059, 6376, 6383, 6508, 6589, 6605, 6892.

[31] Sbaralea, *Bullarium Franciscanum*, I, 442, No. 175.

[32] *Les registres d'Innocent IV, Bibl. des écoles franc.*, No. 5200.

[33] *Les registres de Nicholas IV, Bibl. des écoles franc.*, No. 2057.

bade, under various penalties, marriages of relatives up to and including first cousins, although the rigor of this provision was relaxed after the time of Constantine. The passages of scripture dealing with marriage among relatives were inconsistent, but by allegorically interpreting passages that enjoined marriages of relatives to mean that Christians should only marry those of like faith, the inconsistencies were avoided.

The position of St. Augustine was of great importance in fixing the subsequent attitude of the Church. He held that by marital unions between persons of different kindreds the bonds of Christian charity would be multiplied, and this explanation was adopted by the later canonists to justify the impediment of relationship.

A large number of synodal and conciliar enactments were issued forbidding the marriage of relatives, and many papal decretals supplemented their action. The seventh degree usually was stipulated as the limit of the prohibition, and this limit doubtless was suggested by the Roman law of intestate succession. The method of computing the degree of kinship caused a considerable amount of difficulty, and it was not until the time of Alexander III that the method of counting one generation to a degree was generally adopted. The acceptance of this procedure, together with the mitigation of the rigor of the law by the Fourth Lateran Council which imposed the fourth degree as the limit of the prohibition, placed the law on a much firmer basis.

There were many instances of papal intervention to secure enforcement of the law. The popes usually took action in response to the appeal of the parties or at the behest of the local ecclesiastical authorities who were unable to terminate the case because of interpretative difficulties involved. In some cases, notably those involving Lothair II and Philip Augustus, the local clergy were prevented from impartially enforcing the law because of royal coercion. In practically every instance the popes were found on the side of equity. While not oblivious to the possibility of enhancing papal prestige by securing the capitulation of important offenders, the dictates of justice and the desire of upholding the law of the Church were always prime factors in actuating the pontiffs to intervene in marital cases. In some instances excommunication and interdict were needed to coerce recalcitrant violators of the law; in other cases prompt application of such measures was prevented by the necessity of preserving the support of the personages involved for other projects deemed salutary to the Church and religion. Often obedience to papal mandates could only be secured after a protracted struggle, but in virtually every instance compliance with the law ultimately was attained.

If the number of instances of enforcement of the law is compared with the instances of relaxation, the latter considerably exceed the former. It was comparatively easy to secure dispensations authorizing marriages with relatives in the fourth degree. Dispensations were also occasionally granted for relatives in the third degree, but only when exceptional circumstances seemed to justify such action. Relaxations of the law were extended at first hesitantly and sparingly. Innocent III, however, did not hesitate to grant dispensations where the marriages thus permitted promised to facilitate the attainment of objectives considered beneficial to the Church. The precedents established by Innocent were followed and enlarged upon by his successors. Dispensations were granted to individuals whose devotion the popes were anxious to secure and where the exercise of the dispensing power promised to strengthen papal policies. Dispensations were also granted to stabilize peace between countries and to mitigate the destructiveness of private warfare or to obviate the possibility of the recurrence of such conflicts. Often, however, the motive for granting dispensation was simply a consideration of equity.

Towards the close of the period a number of dispensations were granted to nonnobles as matters of routine, and the ostensible reason for such concessions was usually stated to be either the desire to preserve peace or reluctance to impose hardship on parties who had contracted illegal marriage in ignorance of the law or of the existence of relationship between them. By the pontificate of Boniface IX (1389–1404) compositions were paid to the Papal Curia for marital dispensations,[34] and these represented payments over and above the fees charged for the preparation of the necessary documents. The amount of the fees also was graduated in accordance with the importance of the concession granted.[35] It must be remembered that the law was constantly violated on the manors among the peasantry, who were

---

[34] W. E. Lunt, *Papal Revenues in the Middle Ages* (New York, 1934), I, 132. Fees for matrimonial dispensations were fixed in the *Liber Taxarum Cancellariae Apostolicae. Ibid.*, II, 505, 522.

[35] A. C. Flick, *The Decline of the Medieval Church* (New York, 1930), I, 126.

encouraged or even required to marry someone from their own manor. This condition seems to have been accepted and the violation of the law involved was in most instances tacitly condoned.

BIBLIOGRAPHY

The Roman Law

Codex Justinianus (ed. Krüger), Berlin, 1922.
Codex Theodosianus (ed. Mommsen and Meyer), Leipzig, 1907.
Digesta Justiniana (ed. Mommsen and Krüger), Berlin, 1922.
Gaius, *Institutiones* (ed. Kubler), Teubner, 1928.
Paulus, *Libri Quinque Sententiarum* (ed. Krüger), Berlin, 1878.
Plutarchus, *Quaestiones Romanae* (ed. Rose), Oxford, 1924.
Tacitus, *Annales* (ed. Furneaux), Oxford, 1907.

The Teutonic Law

Edictus Rothari, in *Monumenta Germaniae Historica, Leges*, IV.
Lex Wisigothorum, in *M.G.H., Leges*, I.

The Canon Law

Ambrosius, *Epistolae*, in J. P. Migne (ed.), *Patrologiae Cursus Completus Series Latina*, 221 vols. (Paris, 1844–1855), XCI.
Augustinus, *De Civitate Dei*, in *Corpus Scriptorum Ecclesiasticorum Latinorum*, 65 vols. (Vienna, 1866–), XV.
Benedictus Levita, *Capitularium*, in *M.G.H., Leges*, II.
Bernardus Papiensis, *Summa* (ed. Laspeyres), Ratisbon, 1860.
Burchardus Wormaiensis, *Decretum*, in Migne, *P.L.*, CXL.
Corpus Juris Canonici (ed. Friedberg), Leipzig, 1881.
Decretales Pseudo-Isidorianae et Capitula Angilramni (ed. Hinschius), Leipzig, 1863.
Isidorus, *Etymologiae* (ed. Lindsay), Oxford, 1911.
Ivo Carnotensis, *Decretum*, in Migne, *P.L.*, CLXI.

Jona Aurelianensis, *De Institutione Laicali*, in Migne, *P.L.*, CVI.

Magister Rolandus, *Summa* (ed. Thaner), Innsbruck, 1874.

Petrus Damianus, *De Parentelae Gradibus*, in Migne, *P.L.*, CXLV.

Petrus Lombardus, *Libri Quatuorum Sententiarum*, in Migne, *P.L.*, CXCII.

Rabanus Maurus, *Tractatus de Consanguineorum Nuptiis*, in Migne, *P.L.*, CX.

Stephanus Tornacensis, *Epistolae*, in Migne, *P.L.*, CCXI.

———, *Summa* (ed. Schulte), Giessen, 1891.

CHURCH COUNCILS

Aguirre, J. (ed.), *Collectio Maxima Conciliorum Omnium Hispaniae*, 6 vols. (Ibarra, 1785).

Harduin, J. (ed.), *Conciliorum Collectio regia maxima*, 12 vols. (Paris, 1715).

Hefele, C. J. von, *Conciliengeschichte*, 6 vols. (Freiburg, 1873).

Hefele and Leclerq, H., *Histoire des conciles*, 8 vols. (Paris, 1907).

Mansi, J. D. (ed.), *Sacrorum Conciliorum nova et amplissima Collectio*, 31 vols. (Florence, Venice, 1759–1798).

PAPAL REGISTERS

Bibliothèque des écoles françaises d'Athènes et de Rome:
  Les registres d'Alexandre IV (eds. Bourel, Ronciere, de Loye, Coulon), Paris, 1902–1917.
  Les registres de Boniface VIII (eds. Digard, Faucon, Thomas), Paris, 1884–1921.
  Les registres de Clement IV (ed. Jordan), Paris, 1893–1904.
  Les registres de Grégoire IX (ed. Auvray), Paris, 1896–1908.
  Les registres de Grégoire X (ed. Guiraud), Paris, 1892–1908).
  Les registres de Honorius IV (ed. Prou), Paris, 1888.
  Les registres d'Innocent IV (ed. Berger), Paris, 1884–1911.

Les registres de Martin IV (eds. membres de l'école), Paris, 1901–1913.

Les registres de Nicholas III (ed. Gay), Paris, 1898–1916.

Les registres de Nicholas IV (ed. Langlois), Paris, 1886–1905.

Les registres d'Urbain IV (eds. Dorez and Guiraud), Paris, 1901–1906.

Caspar, E. (ed.), *Gregorii VII Registrum* (Berlin, 1907).

Jaffé, P., *Regesta Pontificum Romanorum*, 2 vols. (Leipzig, 1885).

Potthast, A., *Regesta Pontificum Romanorum*, 2 vols. (Berlin, 1875).

Papal Letters

Bouquet, M. (ed.), *Recueil des historiens des Gaules et de la France*, 24 vols. (Paris, 1900–1904):
Coelestinus II, XV.
Eugenius II, XV.
Lucius II, XV.
Paschalus II, XV.
Urbanus II, XIV.

Migne, *P.L.*:
Adrianus II, CXXII.
Alexandrus II, CXLVI.
Clement III, CCIV.
Gregorius II, LXXXIX.
Honorius III, CCXVI.
Innocentius III, CCXIV–CCXVII.
Leo IV, CXV.
Nicholas I, CXIX.
Vigilius I, LXIX.
Zacharius I, LXXXIX.

Other Papal Letters Cited from the Following

Baluze, S. (ed.), *Miscellanea*, 4 vols. (Luca, 1761–1764).

Boczek, A. (ed.), *Codex diplomaticus et epistolaris Moraviae*, 7 vols. (Prague, 1836–1864).

Böhmer, J. F. (ed.), *Regesta Imperii*, 5 vols. (Stuttgart, 1870).

Devic, C. and Vaisette, J., *Histoire générale de Languedoc*, 16 vols. in 18 (Toulouse, 1872–1905).

Dumont, J. (ed.), *Corps universel diplomatique du droit des gens*, 8 vols. (Amsterdam, 1726–1731).

Finke, H. (ed.), *Acta Aragonensia*, 4 vols. (Berlin, 1908).

Florez, H. (ed.), *España sagrada. Theatro geogr.-historico de la iglesia de España*, 50 vols. (Madrid, 1754–1866).

Gallia Christiana (Paris, 1874), XI.

Huillard-Bréholles, J.L.A. (ed.), *Historia Diplomatica Friderici II*, 7 vols. (Paris, 1852–1861).

Jaffé, P. (ed.), *Bibliotheca Rerum Germanicarum*, 6 vols. (Berlin, 1869).

Jubainville, H. A. de, *Histoire des ducs et des comtes de Champagne*, 5 vols. (Paris, 1859–1869).

Kopp, J., *Geschichte der eidgenössischen Bünde*, 12 vols. (Vienna, 1851).

Langebek, J. (ed.), *Scriptores Rerum Danicarum*, 8 vols. (Hafnia, 1772–1834).

Lettenhove, L. Kervyn de, *Histoire de Flandre*, 6 vols. (Brussels, 1847–1855).

Liljegren, J. (ed.), *Svenskt Diplomatarium*, 5 vols. in 8 (Stockholm, 1829–1867).

Martène, E. (ed.), *Thesaurus novus Anecdotorum*, 5 vols. (Paris, 1717).

Meerman, J., *Geschiednis van Graaf Willem van Holland, Roomsch Koning*, 8 vols. (Gravenhaag, 1783–1797).

Riedel, A. F. (ed.), *Codex Diplomaticus Brandenburgensis*, 3 vols. (Berlin, 1838–1869).

Ripoll, T. (ed.), *Bullarium Ordinis Fratrum Praedicatorum*, 8 vols. (Rome, 1729–1740).

Rördam, H. F. (ed.), *Ny kirkehistoriske Samlinger*, 3 vols. (Copenhagen, 1864–1866).

Rymer, T. (ed.), *Foedera et Acta Publica*, 10 vols. (London, 1816).

Sbaralea, J. (ed.), *Bullarium Franciscanum Romanorum Pontificum*, 4 vols. (Rome, 1759–1768).

Suhm, P., *Historie af Danemark*, 14 vols. (Copenhagen, 1782–1828).

Teulet, A. (ed.), *Layettes du trésor des chartes*, 2 vols. (Paris, 1863–1866).

Theiner, A. (ed.), *Vetera Monumenta Hibernorum et Scotorum Historiam Illustrantia* (Rome, 1864).

——, *Vetera Monumenta Historica Hungariam Sacram Illustrantia*, 2 vols. (Rome, 1859).

——, *Vetera Monumenta Poloniae et Lithuaniae Gentiumque Finitimarum Historiam Illustrantia*, 4 vols. (Rome, 1860).

——, *Vetera Monumenta Slavorum Meridionalium Historiam Illustrantia* (Rome, 1863).

OTHER LETTERS

Deslisle, L. (ed.), *Catalogue des actes de Philippe Auguste* (Paris, 1856).

Epistolae Sancti Abbonis, in *R.H.F.*, X.

Guillelmus Abbas, *Epistolae*, in Langebek, *Scriptores Rerum Danicarum*, VI.

Ingeburga, *Epistolae*, in Langebek, *Scriptores Rerum Danicarum*, VI.

Ivo Carnotensis, *Epistolae*, in Migne, *P.L.*, CXLI.

Suger, *Epistolae*, in *R.H.F.*, XV.

CONTEMPORARY LIVES

Constantinus, *Vita Adalberonis*, in *M.G.H.*, *SS.*, IV.

Gesta Innocentii Tercii, in Migne, *P.L.*, CCXIV.

Guillelmus Zamorae, *Vita Alfonsi IX, Boletin de la Real Academia de la Historia*, XIII.

Hariulfus, *Vita Beati Arnulfi*, in *R.H.F.*, XIV.

Helgaldus Floriacensis, *Vita Roberti Regis*, in *R.H.F.*, X.

Historia Gloriosi Regis Ludovici VII, in *Collection des textes pour servir à l'étude et à l'enseignement de l'histoire*, IV.

Vita Bernardi Tyronensis, in *R.H.F.*, XIV.

Vita Lanfranci (ed. Giles), London, 1887.
Vita Nicholai Papae, in *Liber Pontificalis* (ed. Duchesne), Paris, 1886–1892.
Vita Pontificum, in *M.G.H., SS.,* XX.
Vita Sancti Abbonis, in Migne, *P.L.,* CXXXIX.
Vita Sancti Hilarii Pictavensis, in *R.H.F.,* XIV.

ANNALS AND CHRONICLES, ETC.

Ademarus, *Chronica*, in *Coll. des textes*, XX.
Annales Aquicinctensis, in *R.H.F.,* XVIII.
Annales Colonienses Maximi, in *M.G.H., SS.,* XVII.
Annales Elnonenses, in *M.G.H., SS.,* XVII.
Annales Fuldenses, in *M.G.H., SS.,* I.
Annales Hincmari, in *M.G.H., SS.,* I.
Arnoldus Lubecensis, *Chronica Slavorum*, in *M.G.H., SS.,* XXI.
Bertholdus Constantiensis, *Chronica*, in *R.H.F.,* XIV.
Canonicorum Pragensium Continuatio Cosmae, in *M.G.H., SS.,* XVII.
Chronica Albici Monachi Trium Fontium, in *M.G.H., SS.,* XXIII.
Chronica Sancti Petri Vivi Senonensis, in *R.H.F.,* XII.
Chronicon Malleacensi, in *R.H.F.,* XII.
Chronicon Turonensis, in *R.H.F.,* XII.
Cortes de los antiguos reinos de Leon y de Castilla, 4 vols. (Madrid, 1861).
Extraits des chroniques de S. Denis, in *R.H.F.,* XVII.
Genealogiae Comitum Flandriae, in *M.G.H., SS.,* IX.
Geoffrey Malaterra, *Chronica*, in *R.H.F.,* XIII.
Gerlacus, *Chronicon sive Annales Bohemiae*, in *M.G.H., SS.,* XVII.
Gesta Consulum Andegavensium, in *R.H.F.,* XII.
Gesta Episcoporum Halberstadensium, in *M.G.H., SS.,* XXIII.
Gesta Francorum (*De Gestis Francorum*), in *R.H.F.,* XII.
Gilbertus Montensis, *Chronica*, in *M.G.H., SS.,* XXI.

Guillelmus Armoricus, *Gesta Philippi Augusti, Libraire de la société de l'histoire de France*, II.

Guillelmus de Nangiaco, *Chronica*, in *R.H.F.*, XX.

Guillelmus Malmsburgensis, *De Gestis Regum Anglorum; Historiae Novellae, Rolls Series*.

Guillelmus Neubrigensis, *Historia Anglicana, R.S.*

Heinricus Heimburgensis, *Annales*, in *M.G.H., SS.*, XVII.

Hincmarus, *De Divortio Lotharii et Tetbergae*, in Migne, *P.L.*, CXXV.

Historiae Francicae Fragmentum, in *R.H.F.*, X.

Hugo Flaviniacensis, *Chronica*, in *M.G.H., SS.*, VII.

Jacobus de Guisia, *Annales Hanoniae*, in *M.G.H., SS.*, XXX.

Luca Tudensis, *Chronicon Mundi*, in A. Schottus (ed.), *Hispaniae Illustratae* (Frankfort, 1606), IV.

Mabillon, J. (ed.), *Annales Ordinis Sancti Benedicti*, 6 vols. (Paris, 1703).

Ordericus Vitalis, *Ecclesiastica Historia, Soc. hist. Fr.*

Ottonis Frisingensis Continuatio Sanblasiana, in *M.G.H., SS.*, XX.

Radulfus de Coggeshall, *Chronicon Anglicanum, R.S.*

Radulphus de Diceto, *Ymagines Historiarum, R.S.*

Raynaldus, *Annales ecclesiastici ab a. 1198* (ed. Mansi), Luca, 1747–1756.

Regino Prumiensis Abbatis, *Chronicon*, in *M.G.H., SS.*, I.

Richerus, *Historiarum Libri IV, Soc. hist. Fr.* (Paris, 1845).

Rigordus, *Gesta Philippi Augusti, Soc. hist. Fr.*, II.

Robertus Altissiodoris, *Chronica*, in *R.H.F.*, XVIII.

Rodericus Santus, *Chronica*, in J. Bel (ed.), *Rerum Hispanicarum Scriptores* (Frankfort, 1579).

Rodericus Toletanus, *De Rebus Hispaniae*, in Bel, *Rerum Hispanicarum Scriptores*.

Roger de Hoveden, *Chronica, R.S.*

Rythmus Satyricus de Temporibus Roberti Regis, in *R.H.F.*, X.

Senonensis Chronographus Clarius, in *R.H.F.*, XII.

Sigibertus, *Chronica*, in *M.G.H., SS.*, IV.

Thietmarus, *Chronicon*, in *M.G.H., SS.*, III.

Walterus de Coventria, *Memoriale, R.S.*

Secondary Works

Abella, J., *Manual del matrimonia civil y canonico* (Madrid, 1889).

Achelis, T., *Die Entwicklung der Ehe* (Berlin, 1893).

Aguilar, J., *Procedimientos canonico-civiles respecto a las causas de divorcio y nulidad de matrimonia* (Madrid, 1923).

Brillaud, P. J., *Traité pratique des empêchements et des dispenses de mariage* (Paris, 1871).

Charles, R. H., *Divorce and the Roman Doctrine of Nullity* (Faribault, Minn., 1926).

Corbett, P. E., *The Roman Law of Marriage* (Oxford, 1930).

Esmein, A., *Le mariage en droit canonique*, 2 vols. (Paris, 1891).

Feije, H., *De Impedimentis et Dispensationibus Matrimonialibus* (Louvain, 1885).

Freisen, J., *Das Eheschliessungsrecht* (Paderborn, 1918).

———, *Geschichte des canonischen Eherechts* (Paderborn, 1893).

Gasparri, P., *Tractatus Canonicus de Matrimonio*, 2 vols. (Paris, 1904).

Glasson, E., *Le mariage civil et le divorce dans l'antiquité et dans les principales législations modernes de Europe* (Paris, 1880).

Heiner, F., *Grundriss des katholischen Eherechts* (Münster, 1910).

Leitner, M., *Lehrbuch des katholischen Eherechts* (Paderborn, 1912).

Luckock, H. M., *The History of Marriage Jewish and Christian in Relation to Divorce and Certain Forbidden Degrees* (London, 1895).

McCabe, J., *The Influence of the Church on Marriage and Divorce* (London, 1916).

Morgan, L. H., *Systems of Consanguinity and Affinity of the Human Family* (Washington, 1871).

Preisker, H., *Christentum und Ehe in den ersten drei Jahrhunderte* (Berlin, 1921).

Sohm, R., *Das Recht der Eheschliessung* (Weimar, 1875).

Wake, C. S., *Development of Marriage and Kinship* (London, 1889).

The Following Have Also Been Useful in the Preparation of This Study

Altamira, R., *Historia de España*, 4 vols. (Barcelona, 1928).

Berger, E., *St. Louis et Innocent IV* (Paris, 1893).

Bretholz, B., *Geschichte Böhmens und Mährens bis 1306*, 4 vols. (Munich, 1912).

Cartellieri, A., *Phillipp II August, König von Frankreich*, 4 vols. in 5 (Leipzig, 1899–1902).

Clausen, J., *Papst Honorius III* (Bonn, 1895).

Davidsohn, R., *Philipp II, August von Frankreich und Ingeburg* (Stuttgart, 1888).

Delarc, O., *Saint Grégoire VII et la réforme de l'église* (Paris, 1889).

Fabre, P., "La Pologne et le Saint-Siège du Xe au XIIIe siècle," *Études d'histoire du moyen âge dédiées à Gabriel Monod* (Paris, 1896).

Felten, J., *Papst Gregor IX* (Freiburg, 1886).

Fliche, A., "Hildebrand," *Le Moyen Age*, 2nd series, XXI (1919).

——, *La Réforme grégorienne*, 2 vols. (Paris, 1924–1925).

Flick, A. C., *The Decline of the Medieval Church*, 2 vols. (New York, 1930).

Gay, J., *Les papes du XIe siècle et la chrétienté* (Paris, 1926).

Giesebrecht, W., *Geschichte der Deutschen Kaiserzeit*, 6 vols. (Leipzig, 1877–1895).

Greinacher, A., *Die Anschauungen des Papstes Nikolaus I über das Verhältnis von Staat und Kirche* (Berlin, 1909).

Hauck, A., *Kirchengeschichte Deutschlands*, 5 vols. (Leipzig, 1887–1920).

Hirsch, R., *Studien zur Geschichte König Ludwigs VII von Frankreich* (Leipzig, 1892).

Hurter, F., *Geschichte Papst Innocenz des Dritten*, 4 vols. (Hamburg, 1834).

Lea, H. C., *Studies in Church History* (Philadelphia, 1883).

Lunt, W. E., *Papal Revenues in the Middle Ages*, 2 vols. (New York, 1934).

Mann, H. K., *Lives of the Popes in the Early Middle Ages*, 13 vols. in 14 (St. Louis, 1906–1925).

Martens, W., *Gregor VII, sein Leben und Werken*, 2 vols. (Leipzig, 1894).

Milman, H., *History of Latin Christianity*, 8 vols. (London, 1883).

Palacky, F., *Geschichte von Böhmen*, 4 vols. (Prague, 1845–1874).

Pfister, C., *Études sur le règne de Robert le Pieux* (Paris, 1885).

INDEX

(France), 190; Richard I (England), 114; Robert I (France), 77-83; Sancho (Portugal), 130; Theodebert (Austrasia), 54; Waldemar (Denmark), 187-88; Waldemar (Sweden), 180; William I (England), 16, 157-59; William II (England), 90

Kunigunda, wife of Ottocar II, k. of Bohemia, 188

L

Lanfranc, 158, 159
Laon, Bishop of, 159
Laon, cathedral at, 146
Lateran, councils of, (1123), 17; Fourth (1215), 21-22, 41, 44-45, 53
Lateran palace, meeting of Roman clergy with Nicholas I in, 62, 65, 66
legates, papal, Centius, 110-11; Gualo, 124-25, 126; Guarinus, 126; Hugh of Ostia, 167; John (Nicholas I), 58, 59-60; John of St. Paul's, 119; Octavian (Innocent III), 115-16, 118-19; Octavian (Innocent IV), 175; Peter of Capua, 113-14; Rainerius, 131-32
Le Mans, Bishop of, 89, 90
Leo IV, pope, 19
Leo IX, pope, 15, 157-58
Leopold, duke of Austria, 167-68, 170
Lessines, council of, 12
Leviticus, Book of, 8, 36
Lillebonne, synod of, 16
Limberg, knight of, 175
Limoges, Bishop of, 152
Liutfrid, 56
Liutfrid, brother of Lothair II, k. of Lotharingia, 67
Lombard, Peter, 31-32

London, synods of, (1102), 17; (1125), 17, 40-41; (1200), 41
Lorraine, Charles of, 79
Lothair II, k. of Lotharingia, marital case of, 55-76, marries Teutberga, 55; dismisses Teutberga, 55; marries Waldrada, 55; at council of Aix-la-Chapelle, 56-57; receives permission to marry Waldrada at council, 56-57; censured by Nicholas I, 63-64; meets legate Arsenius at Gundulfi, 68; swears to restore Teutberga and dismiss Waldrada, 68; remains with Waldrada, 69; comes to Rome, 74-75; forgiven by Hadrian II, 75; death of, 75; 198
Louis II, Carolingian emperor, 58; protest of deposed archbishops to, 64-65; invasion of Rome by, 65-66; 67; campaign of against Saracens, 73-74
Louis VII, k. of France, 86, 121; marital case of, 159-62, marriage to Eleanor of, 159; crusade of, 159-60; reconciliation of with Eleanor, 160; dissolution of marriage with Eleanor by Council of Beaugency, 161; effects of separation of from Eleanor, 161-62
Louis VIII, k. of France, 153
Louis IX, k. of France, 172, 184
Louis, son of Philip I, k. of France, 85, 96
Louis, son of Philip II, k. of France, 112
Louis, son of Philip IV, k. of France, 190
Louis the German, k. of Austrasia, 61; letter of Nicholas I to, 64; meeting of with Charles the Bald at Tullei, 67; delivery of papal letter to, 68

Rome, synods of, (402), 38; (721-724), 12; (725), 49; (743), 11-12, 38-39; (826), 13, 39-40

Rothschild, Peter, bishop of, 106

Rouen, synod of, 16

Rozala, wife of Robert I of France, 77

Rudolph, patriarch of Jerusalem, 149

S

Saintes, Urban II at, 93

Salamanca, council of, 130

Salisbury, Count of, 145

Salonne, Archbishop of, 162

Salzburg, Archbishop of, 140, 141, 170

Salzburg, synod of, 12

Sancho, k. of Portugal, 130

Sancius, son of Alfonso X, k. of Castile, 154

Saracens, converted, recipients of marital dispensations, 163

Saxony, Duke of, 180

Seligenstadt, synod of, 27

Senlis, Bishop of, 89

Sens, Archbishop of, 91

Sens, Philip I, k. of France, at, 96

Seville, Isidore of, 25

Simon, Cardinal Priest of St. Caecilia, 180-81

Simon de Montfort, 185

Soissons, 60, 127

Soissons, Bishop of, 149

Soissons, clergy of, ordered to coerce Erardus of Brienne, 151

Soissons, council of, 117, 118-19

Sophia, niece of King of Denmark, 180

Spain, 153. See Alfonso VIII, Alfonso IX, Alfonso X, Innocent III

spiritual relationship, impediment of, defined, 5; legislation on, 48-51

Stephen, bishop of Noyon, 105

Stephen of Tournai, see Tournai, Stephen of

Stephen VIII, pope, decretal on spiritual relationship of, 50

St. Leodegarius, Ingeburg at, 115-16

St. Stephen Proto-Martyr, monastery of, 158-59

Suger, Abbé, minister of Louis VII, k. of France, 160

Susanna, see Rozala

Swabia, Philip of, 140, 141, 164

Sweden, 180. See Magnus, k. of; Waldemar, k. of

Sybyl, queen of Jerusalem, 148

Sylvester II, pope, see Gerbert, archbishop of Rheims

synod, Aachen, 12-13; Agde, 9-10, 38; Ancyra, 37; Beaugency, 97; Bremen, 22; Cassel, 17; Clermont, 10-11, 38; Compiègne, 12, 39, 49; Douci, 14, 26; Elne, 15; Elvira, 37; Epaon, 10, 38; Freisingen, 12; Garonne, 16; Lillebonne, 16; London (1102), 17, (1125), 17, 40-41, (1200), 41; Mainz, 13; Metz, 59, 61, 62; New Caesarea, 37-38; Orléans (III), 11, 38, (IV), 11, 38; Paris (557), 11, 38, (829), 13; Riesbach, 12; Rome (402), 38, (721-724), 12, (725), 49, (743), 11-12, 38-39, (826), 13, 39-40; Rouen, 16; Salzburg, 12; Seligenstadt, 27; Toledo, 10; Torcello, 22; Toul, 11; Tours, 13; Tribur, 40; Trosle, 14; Trullan, 11, 48-49; Vermeria, 39; Vienne and Tours, 16-40; Worms, 13, 40, 49

T

Tacitus, quoted, 6

Teutberga, wife of Lothair II, k. of Lotharingia, 55-76, marries Lothair, 55; charges against, 55; separated from Lothair by Council of Aix-la-Chapelle, 57; promised restoration as wife, 68; coerced by Lothair, 70; petitions pope to dissolve her marriage, 70; reply of Nicholas I to, 70-71; received by Hadrian II at Rome, 72-73

Texa, 155

Theobald of Champagne, see Champagne, Theobald of

Theodebert, k. of Austrasia, 54

Theodosius, Roman emperor, 7, 35

Theresa, daughter of King of Portugal, 130, 131

Thietgaudus, archbishop of Trèves, 56; comes to Rome, 61-62; deposed by Nicholas I, 62; defies pope, 64; protests to Louis II, 64-65; vainly seeks reinstatement, 66

Thuringia, Landgrave of, 173-74

Toledo, Archbishop of, 135

Toledo, second synod of, 10

Tongherne, Franconus, bishop of, 66

Torcello, synod of, 22

Torres, 169

Torres, Archbishop of, 144

Torres, Judge of, 168

Toul, synod of, 11

Toulouse, Raymond of, 172-73

Tournai, Stephen of, 32; Summa of, 32-33; 108

Tours, Berengar of, 158

Tours, council of, 93

Tours, Philip I, k. of France, at, 87

Tours, synod of, 13

Trèves, Thietgaudus, archbishop of, 56

Tribur, synod of, 40

Trosle, synod of, 14

Troyes, assembly of French clergy at, 92

Troyes, council of, 96-97

Trullan synod, 11, 48-49

Tübingen, Count Palatine of, 178

Tullei, meeting of Charles the Bald and Louis the German at, 67

Tusculum, reconciliation of Louis VII and Eleanor at, 160

Tyre, county of, 149

U

Ulric of Carinthia, 175

Urban II, pope, 16; enforcement of marital laws against Philip I, k. of France, 89-94, letter to Archbishop of Rheims of, 89; letters to and from Ivo of Chartres, 91-92; policy of at Council of Clermont, 92-93; attendance of at Council of Tours, 93; Council of Nîmes held by, 93; absolution of Philip I by, 94; death of, 94

Urban IV, pope, dispensations issued by, 180-81, 186, 197

V

Valentinian I, Roman emperor, 35

Veranus, Quintus, 6

Verberie, synod of, see Vermeria

Verino, Peter of, 195

Vermeria, synod of, 39

Vienne, interdict on France proclaimed at, 114

Vienne and Tours, synod of, 16, 40

Vigilius I, pope, 54